Cumbria Way

Paddy Dillon

Rucksack Readers

Cumbria Way: a Rucksack Reader

Second, revised edition published in 2021 by Rucksack Readers, 6 Old Church Lane, Edinburgh, EH15 3PX, UK; first edition published 2013 in another format.

Phone   +44/0131 661 0262

Email: **info@rucsacs.com**

Website   *www.rucsacs.com*

ISBN 978-1-913817-03-9

British Library Cataloguing in Publication Data: a catalogue record for this book is available from the British Library.

Designed in Scotland by Ian Clydesdale (ian@clydesdale.scot)

Printed in the UK by Short Run Press, Exeter on rainproof, biodegradable paper

FSC
www.fsc.org
MIX
Paper from
responsible sources
FSC® C014540

Publisher's note

All information was checked prior to publication, but at a time when England was still emerging from its latest lockdown due to the global pandemic. We cannot know which of the facilities that we list and show on mapping will survive and you need to check before relying on any. Always take local advice and look out for signage e.g. for diversions. Check two websites for updates before setting out: *bit.ly/cumbriaway* and *www.rucsacs.com/books/cbr*.

The weather in Cumbria is unpredictable year-round, and parts of the Way are exposed, remote, and wet underfoot. You are responsible for your own safety, and for ensuring that your clothing, food and equipment are suited to your needs. The publisher cannot accept any liability for any ill-health, accident or loss arising directly or indirectly from reading this book.

Feedback is welcome and will be rewarded

We are grateful to readers for comments and suggestions. All feedback will be followed up, and readers whose comments lead to changes will be entitled to claim a free copy of our next edition upon publication. Please send emails to *info@rucsacs.com*.

Contents

Foreword

If there's one walk that captures the sheer variety of the Lakeland landscape, this is it. The peace and quiet of the Blawith Fells, bustling Coniston, picturesque Tarn Hows, the challenge of Stake Pass from Langdale over to Langstrath, Borrowdale, Derwent Water, Back o' Skiddaw and the river valley approaches to Carlisle. Who could ask for more?

Me. I have to confess that I'm by nature a diverter and if you're not pushed for time, the Cumbria Way provides the perfect backbone to an exploration of a wider Lakeland – the views from the pretend lighthouse on Hoad Hill above Ulverston; The Cathedral, a spectacular slate cavern out by Tilberthwaite; the prehistoric equivalent of the iPhone at Castlerigg stone circle above Keswick – calculator, calendar, clock and messaging service all rolled into one; the atmospheric, abandoned bobbin mill in The Howk at Caldbeck; and dozens more such side-trips.

But if your time is limited, come back to see all those things another day, and in the meantime relish five or six days of relatively gentle walking. In fact, if you're new to long distance walking, this is the perfect introduction. The only real challenges are on the long haul from Mickleden up to Stake Pass, and the high-level route over the summit of High Pike. The rest of the seventy-plus miles you can devote to inspirational thoughts – such as wanting to strangle the man who wrote the Foreword when you get caught in a downpour in Langstrath (as I did) or go up to your hocks in the bogs o' Skiddaw (as I did).

But look on the bright side. I promise you will dry out – eventually.

Eric Robson

Chairman of Cumbria Tourism and the Wainwright Society

Through Mickleden towards Stake Pass

1 Planning

Best time of year

The earliest that most walkers attempt the Cumbria Way is Easter – anywhere from late March to late April, when wintry conditions are still possible. Springtime, April to mid May, can feature cool, clear weather, with the first flowers appearing, trees just coming into leaf and newborn lambs in the lower pastures. It might still snow, but snow will seldom lie on the ground.

Early summer, mid May to June, looks much greener, with the trees covered in leaves, bracken growing on rugged fellsides, and plenty of flowers in bloom. Sheep are moved onto rough grazing on the high fells. Midsummer, July and August, tends to be warmer, but is also the busiest time in the Lake District, when accommodation fills up. The weather can be good, but it is essential still to be prepared for rain and wind, especially in exposed parts of the route.

September and October generally see fairly settled weather, often with wonderful autumn red, brown and gold colours as the foliage begins to turn. As the weather gets colder, it may snow on higher ground. The winter months, November to March, are suitable only if you can take advantage of clear weather at short notice. Even hardy Herdwick sheep are no longer on the fells. Stake Pass and the Northern Fells can be difficult to cross if covered in snow and ice, and daylight hours are very limited. If you live locally, you may seize the odd clear, crisp day, but winter is not a good time to plan an expedition from afar.

Regardless of season, what really matters is the weather for each day you spend on the route. Check specific Lake District forecasts on Weatherline: *www.lakedistrictweatherline.co.uk*. Be warned that the wettest inhabited place in England is at Seathwaite in Borrowdale, barely 4 km from the Cumbria Way at Rosthwaite. And remember that in misty conditions or low cloud, your navigation skills may be tested. See page 71 for recommended maps.

Which direction?

Footbridge over Stake Beck

Most walkers walk south to north, from Ulverston to Carlisle, in the hope that any wet or windy weather will come from behind them. This guidebook is arranged in this direction, and anyone walking the reverse way will have to take great care to follow the route description 'backwards'. Finishing in a city such as Carlisle means having more facilities and better onward transport links than in a smaller town such as Ulverston. However, the minority who choose to walk from north to south will find adequate facilities there, and those who have already walked the Way may enjoy the different views.

Getting there and away

Almost 90% of visitors reach the Lake District by car, but this is not the best way to reach a long-distance walk. Arriving at one end of the route, you would need to find secure parking for a week, then after walking you would have to return for the car.

Ulverston and Carlisle are both served by rail, with excellent links to the rest of Britain. There are direct daily rail services to Ulverston from Manchester Airport, and regular daily links between Lancaster, on the West Coast Mainline, and Ulverston. Carlisle has excellent daily rail links with London, Birmingham, Leeds, Newcastle upon Tyne, Glasgow and Edinburgh. For National Rail Enquiries, see page 70.

National Express coaches are very cheap when booked in advance. Many services call at Carlisle, along with Scottish Citylink services. Ulverston isn't on a coach route, but Kendal is, and the X6 Stagecoach bus runs daily from Kendal to Ulverston. Links for National Express and Citylink are provided on page 70.

Every stage of the Cumbria Way is served by buses, mainly operated by Stagecoach. Most of these run daily, but a few don't run on Sundays, and some services are infrequent. The main bus transport hubs are Ulverston, Ambleside (for Coniston and Langdale), Keswick and Carlisle: for information refer to Traveline. Contact details for boat trips on the lakes, as well as for Traveline, are on page 70.

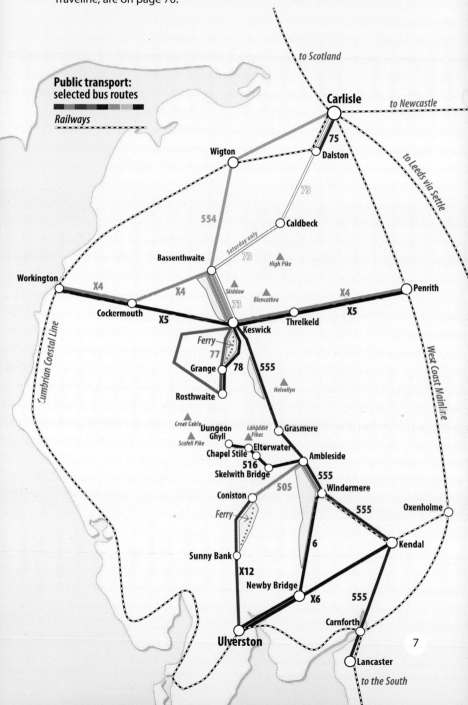

Public transport: selected bus routes

Railways

How long will it take?

Table 1 Distances and overnight stops. Total (all itineraries): 73·3mi 117·9km

	Ulverston	Sunny Bank	Coniston	Elterwater	Dungeon Ghyll	Rosthwaite	Keswick	Skiddaw Hse	Caldbeck	Dalston	Carlisle
5 days (mi)		15·7		11·6		15·5		15·0		15·5	
5 days (km)		25·2		18·7		24·9		24·1		25·0	
6 days (mi)		15·7		11·6	7·3	8·2		15·0		15·5	
6 days (km)		25·2		18·7	11·7	13·2		24·1		25·0	
7 days (mi)	11·9	3·8	7·9		11·0	8·2		15·0		15·5	
7 days (km)	19·1	6·1	12·7		17·7	13·2		24·1		25·0	
10 days (mi)	11·9	3·8	7·9	3·7	7·3	8·2	5·6	9·4	10·0	5·5	
10 days (km)	19·1	6·1	12·7	6·0	11·7	13·2	9·0	15·1	16·2	8·8	

Most walkers need at least five full days for the Cumbria Way. This guidebook describes the route in six sections, but the two shortest stages can be combined. For a distance of 73½ miles (118 km), a six-day itinerary averages out at about 12 miles (19.3 km) per day. In practice, you will walk a bit further because you'll have to go off-route to find food, drink, and accommodation. The low-level alternative from Keswick to Caldbeck would add an extra 3 miles (5 km). Most people will do at least 80 miles/130 km in all.

Bear in mind that the first and last days are mainly in farmland, with lots of stiles and gates that take time to negotiate. Avoid the temptation to arrive in Ulverston mid-morning in the hope of being able to walk all the way to Coniston: this could result in a very late finish. Better to spend a night in town and make an early start the next morning. On the final day, avoid trying to rush from Caldbeck to Carlisle in the hope of catching a train home. Much better to overnight and explore the city the next day, and travel home at leisure. Allow at least a week to enjoy walking the Way.

Most walkers start on Saturday, but bear in mind that Ulverston is a 'Festival Town', with events on most weekends through the summer. Also, the Lake District is a very popular destination, and in high summer it can be difficult to secure lodgings. Arriving mid-week in Coniston, Langdale and Keswick is less likely to lead to booking problems. Accommodation in the little village of Caldbeck is very limited, and it may be worth securing a bed there first.

The Way visits interesting towns and villages such as Ulverston, Coniston and Keswick. To explore them properly you need a few free hours in each. To reach museums within opening hours, re-organise your schedule to include half-day walks, leaving mornings or afternoons free for visits. Table 1 suggests five, six, seven and ten-day schedules.

Accommodation

There is a wide range of accommodation – from simple campsites to expensive hotels – but it is unevenly spread along the Way. There is no on-route accommodation between Ulverston and Coniston to break the first long day. Between Coniston and Great Langdale, there are several intermediate lodgings. After a long gap, options are dotted throughout Borrowdale. The town of Keswick has many places to stay, whilst to its north there is only Skiddaw House Youth Hostel in the middle of the Northern Fells. Caldbeck has very limited accommodation, whereas at the finish, the city of Carlisle offers plenty of choice.

Many walkers are happy to book all their overnights themselves from a list. You are strongly advised to book well in advance. Some are happy to use a Tourist Information Centre to make their bookings, whilst others prefer to let a tour company take care of everything including baggage transfers. All

Facilities along the Way

This list was finalised at a time when England was still emerging from its latest lockdown due to the global pandemic. Check which facilities are open before relying on any.

	miles from last place	km from last place	café, pub, restaurant	shop	campsite	hostel, barn, bunkhouse	B&B/hotel
Ulverston			✓	✓	✓		✓
Lowick Bridge 2 km			✓				✓
Torver 2·5 km			✓		✓		✓
Coniston Hall	14·7	23·6		✓	✓		
Coniston	1·0	1·6	✓	✓		✓	✓
High Park	4·9	7·9	✓				
Elterwater Park	0·9	1·5	✓				✓
Skelwith Bridge 400 m			✓		✓		✓
Elterwater	2·1	3·3	✓			✓	✓
Chapel Stile	0·5	0·8	✓	✓	✓		
Robinson Place 900 m							✓
New Dungeon Ghyll	2·3	3·7	✓				✓
Old Dungeon Ghyll	0·9	1·5	✓	✓	✓		✓
Stonethwaite 200 m			✓		✓		✓
Rosthwaite	7·3	11·7	✓			✓	✓
Hollows Farm Campsite	1·7	2·7			✓		
Grange 600 m			✓				✓
Nichol End 200 m			✓				
Portinscale	5·4	8·7	✓				✓
Keswick	1·1	1·8	✓	✓	✓	✓	✓
Skiddaw House *	5·6	9·0				✓	
Mosedale 3 km							✓
Hudscales 1·5 km						✓	
Caldbeck *	9·4	15·1	✓	✓	✓		✓
Bridge End	9·1	14·6	✓				
Dalston	1·0	1·6	✓	✓	✓		✓
Cummersdale 600 m			✓				
Carlisle	5·4	8·8	✓	✓		✓	✓

* Between Skiddaw House and Caldbeck, those following the low-level alternative route can divert for facilities (pub, B&B) at Bassenthwaite (1·6 km off-route) or Uldale (2 km off-route).
Places that are off-route are shown in italics with distance off-route after placename.

these approaches are fine, but remember that the Lake District gets very busy during the summer, especially at weekends, and some places fill up quickly.

If you can't secure lodgings on route for every night, don't despair. Most of the Way is well served by bus services: see page 7. With careful planning, you can complete a day's walk and still catch a bus to your accommodation. For example, if Coniston is full, take a bus back to Ulverston or go off-route to Ambleside. Langdale also has a good bus link with Ambleside. Walkers who want to stop in Borrowdale but are unable to find lodgings can easily catch a bus to Keswick, then return and pick up the route the following day. Caldbeck has only limited bus services, but they connect with both Keswick and Carlisle.

Some walkers like to camp, while others prefer hostels, and many are happy also to stay at B&Bs or hotels. Sticking to a certain type of accommodation may require alterations to the schedule. There is no hostel at the head of Great Langdale, for example, so hostellers would have either to finish early at Elterwater, or pass through the village on the way to the Old Dungeon Ghyll Hotel, then catch a bus back to Elterwater.

Food and drink is available from shops, pubs and cafés at many points along the route, but there are long gaps with no facilities. Many towns and villages offer an excellent range, but there are also isolated pubs, farmhouse tearooms and other options along the Way: refer to the facilities table on page 9.

Waymarking and navigation

Throughout the Lake District, public rights of way are well marked where they leave roads, but less well marked in fields and on open fellside. The southernmost part of the Way between Ulverston and Gawthwaite, is sometimes signposted as such. Mostly, however, the words 'Cumbria Way' are written very small and set into waymark arrows on small plastic discs. Watch carefully to spot these, especially when the Cumbria Way intersects with other waymarked public footpaths and bridleways. Many of the markers are faded or damaged, so the words are not always legible.

In some instances, landowners have created their own Cumbria Way signs. A few are very clear, but many are low-key, faded or overgrown with foliage. Watch carefully to spot waymarks, particularly when passing through farmyards, where there might be several gates but only one way through. The least well marked stretch of the route is from Keswick to Caldbeck on the high-level main route, with markers sometimes literally miles apart. We recommend you carry and consult a large-scale map: see page 71.

Considerable stretches of the Way run through low-level farmland where fields are separated by drystone walls and post-and-wire fences. These boundaries are crossed using a variety of stiles, many of which bear Cumbria Way marker discs. Stiles come in all shapes and sizes: gap-stiles are narrow gaps in walls, barely wide enough for walkers to squeeze their legs through, and often a challenge for large dogs. Step-stiles range from planks of wood arranged to let you step over a fence to a series of stone steps projecting through a drystone wall, running up one side and down the other. Ladder-stiles are usually made of timber and used to cross walls or fences.

Where a stile is next to an unlocked gate, you may prefer to use the gate rather than the stile, especially if walking as a group or with dogs: but it is essential to close the gate securely afterwards. Kissing-gates allow one person at a time to pass through, but keep livestock out. Gates on public bridleways are required by law to open and close, but gates on public footpaths can legally be locked, provided that there is a stile alongside. Usually any right of way applies to the stile, not the gate. Some farm roads are equipped with gates to prevent livestock straying. Instead of gates, there may be cattle grids on some roads, although most grids have a gate alongside.

There are a few stretches of the route where waymark discs don't carry the words 'Cumbria Way'. In such places, refer to the map and route description to ensure that you are still on course, and keep an eye on the discs until they carry the name of the route again. If you suspect that you are no longer on route, it is usually better to retrace your steps to the last waymarker than to attempt a short cut across country.

Responsible access and dogs

The Cumbria Way follows a mixture of public footpaths, public bridleways and public byways. Public footpaths are for walkers only. Public bridleways may be used by people travelling on foot, bicycle or horseback. Public byways are open to all bridleway users, and in addition to users of any type of vehicle that fits on the byway unless specifically banned.

Dogs are allowed on all these routes, provided that they are kept under control. Special care must be taken wherever dogs may encounter wildlife or livestock. Dogs can cause stress to ground-nesting birds, sheep and lambs simply by their presence. Large animals, especially cows with calves, may react aggressively to a dog. The National Farmers Union advises that dogs be kept on leads near livestock, but also says that if attacked by cattle a dog should be let off lead. Dog owners have been trampled and killed while trying to protect their dogs, so let your dog go and save yourself as a matter of urgency. Your dog will easily escape and should return to you afterwards.

The Countryside Code was revised in 2021. For a full explanation of everyone's rights and responsibilities see the panel and *www.gov.uk/countryside-code.*

Remoteness and experience

There are only a few places along the Way where walkers lose sight of habitations. These include parts of the Blawith Fells, Stake Pass and parts of the Northern Fells. Most of the time there will be farms and villages nearby, though in well-wooded areas they may not be obvious. Even in the most remote parts of the Northern Fells, escape routes are never far away.

The Cumbria Way is often attempted by walkers with little or no experience of long-distance walking. If this applies to you (or to anybody you are walking with), please consult our *Notes for novices*: see page 71. This will help with realistic planning, and your enjoyment is likely to be greater if you know how to estimate what distance you can comfortably cover in a day.

Countryside Code

Respect everyone
- be considerate to those living in, working in and enjoying the countryside
- leave gates and property as you find them
- do not block access to gateways or driveways when parking
- be nice, say hello, share the space
- follow local signs and keep to marked paths unless wider access is available

Protect the environment
- take your litter home – leave no trace of your visit
- do not light fires and only have BBQs where signs say you can
- always keep dogs under control and in sight
- dog poo – bag it and bin it – any public waste bin will do
- care for nature – do not cause damage or disturbance

Enjoy the outdoors
- check your route and local conditions
- plan your adventure – know what to expect and what you can do
- enjoy your visit, have fun, make a memory

Terrain and gradients

The Cumbria Way starts among farms and fields, then passes through the Lake District National Park. Although there are a number of fairly rugged ascents and descents, the route mostly runs through the dales (valleys). There is little altitude gain in the first section north from Ulverston; the first real climb is to the top of Stake Pass between Great Langdale and Borrowdale. In fine weather this is a splendid hike, but in poor visibility or snow it needs great care to avoid a slip on rugged terrain. After the gentle ground of Borrowdale, the Northern Fells seem wild and exposed. The main route goes over the summit of High Pike, tricky in poor visibility, and we explain on page 52 when to choose the lower-level alternative. The final stage into Carlisle is mostly flat and easy, following riverside paths and tracks.

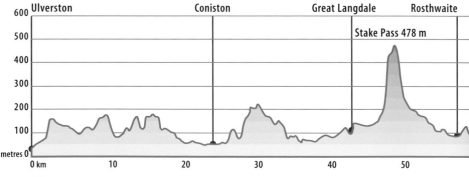

Packing checklist

The checklist below refers to your daytime needs, and is divided into essential and desirable. Experienced walkers may disagree about our categories, but this list makes a starting-point. Normally you will be wearing the first three or four items and carrying the rest in your rucksack.

Essential

- comfortable, waterproof walking boots
- specialist walking socks
- breathable clothing in layers
- waterproof jacket and over-trousers
- hat and gloves
- guidebook, map and compass
- in case of injury, whistle and torch for attracting attention
- water carrier and plenty of water (or purification tablets/drops)
- enough food to last between supply points
- first aid kit including blister treatment
- toiletries and overnight necessities
- insect repellent and sun protection (summer)
- rucksack (at least 35 litres)
- waterproof rucksack cover or liner, e.g. bin (garbage) bag
- enough cash in pounds sterling, with credit/debit card as backup.

Credit cards are not always acceptable and cash machines are sparse along the Way. Bin bags have many uses e.g. store wet clothing or prevent hypothermia.

Desirable

- walking pole(s)
- binoculars: useful for navigation and spotting wildlife
- camera (ideally light and rugged), also spare batteries, memory card or film
- pouch or secure pockets, to keep small items handy but safe
- gaiters (to keep mud and water out of boots)
- toilet tissue (biodegradable)
- small plastic bags for litter
- spare socks: changing socks at lunchtime can relieve damp feet
- spare shoes (e.g. trainers, crocs or sandals)
- towel if hostelling
- notebook and pen
- mobile phone: useful for arrangements but don't rely on one for emergencies. Reception can be patchy.

Camping

If you are camping, you need much more gear, including tent, sleeping gear, camping stove, fuel, cooking utensils and food. Your rucksack will need to be larger e.g. 50-80 litres, and camping could add 5-10 kg to its weight. Previous experience is advisable.

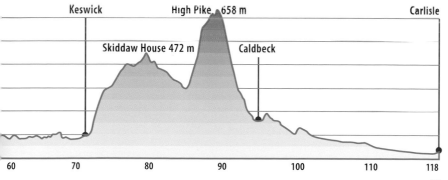

2·1 Geology, scenery and mining

The Cathedral - a quarry in Little Langdale

The 'Cumbria Waymarker' spire contains rocks that represent the geology along the route. At the base of the cage is limestone, with slate in the middle, and red sandstone at the top. This is a useful, albeit oversimplified, mnemonic for the Lake District geology that you encounter from south to north.

The Skiddaw slates are about 500 million years old and were laid down in a shallow sea, but now form one of the highest fells - Skiddaw - which towers above Keswick. The same rock occurs in the north and north-west of the Lake District, as well as further south around Black Combe near Millom, giving rise to smooth, rounded fells.

The Borrowdale volcanic rocks form the rugged, rocky heart of the Lake District and are about 450 million years old. They vary from lava to volcanic ash, forming the highest fells; in some areas they can be quarried and split into thin slabs. Although these slabs are referred to as 'slate', they are not true slates. Some are cut and polished as ornamental stonework.

Cumbria Waymarker, Ulverston

The southern part of the Lake District, between Ulverston and Coniston, is mostly composed of Silurian rocks, about 415 to 445 million years old. They are made up of marine mudstone, flagstone, gritstone and limestone.

Almost the whole Lake District is surrounded by 400 million year old Devonian red sandstone, laid down in desert conditions, and 350 million year old Carboniferous limestone, deposited in a shallow sea. These rock types are thought to have completely covered the Lake District, but were later worn away and now are found only on the fringes of the area.

Roughton Stone, Caldbeck

Vast intrusions of molten granite and gabbro were forced into the bedrock, baking some of the older rocks, squeezing mineral veins into joints and forcing the whole Lake District into a dome. It is rare for granite and gabbro to be found in the same place, but this happens around the Caldbeck Fells, where an amazing range of minerals are found, including rarities found nowhere else in Britain. The location finder on High Pike bears the legend 'Caldbeck and the Caldbeck Fells are worth all England else' and this refers to its mineral wealth. For information about this area, see *bit.ly/caldbeck*.

The Lake District has been mined for iron, lead, copper and wolfram (tungsten). A rare deposit of graphite in Borrowdale was exploited, leading to the creation of the world's first pencils. The western fringes of Cumbria have been extensively mined for coal, the southern fringes for iron, while the eastern fringes are still mined for gypsum. There are still working slate quarries, as well as the massive spoil heaps of long-exhausted quarries.

Despite the varied rock types, the shape of the Lake District was largely determined in the Ice Age, in the last two million years. Look at a map of the Lake District and you'll see that the main lakes are long and slender, and seem to radiate from a centre. William Wordsworth likened them to 'spokes from the nave of a wheel'. Smaller bodies of water, known as 'tarns', number anywhere from 50 to 300, depending on what you count. All these water features, and the valleys they occupy, are the result of glaciers that finally vanished only 10,000 years ago. They scoured the Lake District, deepening the valleys, leaving hollow areas to flood and dumping rubble-like heaps of moraine.

Ancient layers of volcanic ash displayed in slate

2·2 Farming, sheep and the National Park

Farming in the Lake District is overwhelmingly devoted to rearing sheep, and in the central parts to Herdwick sheep in particular. There are few cattle farms, though you walk through a couple at both the beginning and end of the Way. Apart from meadows for grazing, and the production of silage and hay, there is very little arable crop farming until the flat, sandy fields approaching Carlisle.

Although most sheep are grazed on the open fells in summer, they are brought down to the lower fields near the farms for the winter. The fields close to the farms are known as the 'intake', and they are generally surrounded by centuries-old drystone walls. However, some drystone walls also run for miles over rugged fells, leaving many visitors wondering how on earth they were built.

The material for drystone walls lies everywhere – scattered on the fellsides or littering the ground. The true skill of a drystone waller is knowing how to choose and arrange assorted lumps of rock on top of each other so that they remain standing.

The first task is to excavate a trench and lay a line of very large stones as a foundation or 'footing'. Next, two parallel walls are built, leaning slightly into each other. These are bonded every so often by placing a large stone slab horizontally across both walls, known as a 'through' stone. Gaps between the two walls are filled with small stones, sometimes known as 'heartings'. The top of the wall is often finished with a line of protruding stones, or 'cams', to prevent animals from climbing over. The finished wall is, literally, rock solid: each stone is locked in place by the sheer weight of all the rest.

Whenever you pass a collapsed drystone wall, you have a chance to study its internal construction. A demonstration drystone wall can be seen at the Ruskin Museum at Coniston: see page 70.

Drystone-walled sheepfold, Northern Fells

Herdwick sheep

Herdwicks are native to the high fells of the Lake District, and while some say they were introduced by the Vikings, or swam ashore from a sinking Armada vessel, it is more likely they were always present. They have a very strong 'hefting' instinct, which means that they always graze the fellsides that their ancestors grazed, and if moved away, they will always strive to return. They are seen very occasionally on 'rare breed' farms outside the Lake District.

Herdwicks are born very dark brown, almost black, but as they grow up their faces and lower legs turn grey. Eventually, the whole coarse fleece becomes a lighter brown, turning grey as they mature.

Young male lambs are 'wethers' and young females are 'gimmers', and these names occur as place-names around the Lake District. Once separated from their mothers, they are referred to as 'hoggs', and two-year olds are called 'twinters'. Males generally go straight to the slaughter houses, whereas females are kept for further breeding. Older males grow horns and are called 'tips' or 'tups', while older hornless females are 'ewes', often pronounced 'yowes'.

A Herdwick's year is divided into four stages: lambing, shearing, dipping and tipping. Lambing takes place around mid-April. Shearing of older sheep occurs in July, but the coarse wool is almost worthless. Coloured 'smit' or identification marks are put on the sheep afterwards. Dipping takes place in September, to reduce and control insect parasites. Mature male 'tips' are introduced to females from the middle of November for mating, starting the cycle all over again.

Herdwicks used to be put onto the open fell after tipping, but this is no longer done. Instead, they are brought down from the fells and kept on the 'intake' near the farms from mid November to mid May. While this helps with bio-diversity on the fells, it also makes the Herdwick breed less hardy than it used to be.

Counting sheep

Sheep have always been counted in multiples of 20 in the Lake District, and indeed throughout Britain, for centuries. The long-dead language of the Old North (Cumbric) was related to Welsh, Cornish and Breton. It was very seldom written down, except for its counting system. This survived well into the 20th and 21st centuries for counting sheep, in knitting and in nursery rhymes. Cumbrian shepherds still use it to this day, and the word 'yan' for 'one' is widespread in everyday usage. The pronunciation varies locally, but here is an example:

1	yan	5	pimp	9	davera	13	tethera-dick	17	tyan-a-bumfit
2	tyan	6	sethera	10	dick	14	methera-dick	18	tethera-bumfit
3	tethera	7	lethera	11	yan-a-dick	15	bumfit	19	methera-bumfit
4	methera	8	hovera	12	tyan-a-dick	16	yan-a-bumfit	20	giggot

Lake District National Park

In 1810, William Wordsworth wrote his *Guide to the Lakes* for people who 'testify that they deem the district a sort of national property, in which every man has a right and interest who has an eye to perceive and a heart to enjoy'. In effect, he was thinking of the Lake District as a kind of national park long before it was designated as such in 1951. The Lake District National Park celebrated its 70th birthday in 2021, four years after the area was inscribed as a UNESCO World Heritage Site in its Cultural Landscape category.

This is the largest National Park in England, with an area of 912 square miles (2362 square km). Unlike elsewhere in the world, national parks in Britain are not state-owned, but the land is held by many different individuals and organisations. As a result, it is used extensively for various agricultural, industrial and leisure activities. About 40,500 people live within the National Park and two-thirds of its houses are owner-occupied. In 2018 over 19 million people visited the Lake District and the annual number will be higher by the time you read this. The majority are day trippers, but many visitors need to be accommodated as well as fed. This results in an annual spend of over £1.5 billion in the area.

A considerable proportion of the high fells is leased to the National Trust, and the Trust also owns other patches of land, farms, historic buildings, car parks and even operates a pub, the Sticklebarn Tavern in Great Langdale: see *www.nationaltrust.org.uk*.

The Lake District National Park Authority, a politically appointed body, aims to reconcile the various activities that take place in the area. The authority strives to sustain the landscape, wildlife and culture, while at the same time allowing economic development to take place, especially that which benefits local communities: see *www.lakedistrict.gov.uk*.

Middle Fell Farm, a traditional sheep farm, Great Langdale

2·3 History

About 14,650 archaeological sites and monuments have been recorded in the Lake District. There is space here to describe only the background to this rich treasure.

Humans have been living in Cumbria for thousands of years, arriving as Mesolithic hunter-gatherers on the coast. Moving inland, Neolithic stone axe 'factories' were developed in Great Langdale, and the mighty Castlerigg Stone Circle was constructed near Keswick. The western half of the Lake District features a wealth of Bronze Age settlement sites and monuments.

The Romans pushed north through Britain, consolidating their frontier in AD122 by building Hadrian's Wall, as well as a string of forts along the Cumbria coast and in the heart of the Lake District. When the Romans departed in the 5th century, Celtic chieftains ruled, until Angles, Danes and Norse invaders stamped their authority on the area, up to the 10th century. Most old placenames are Norse, though 'Cumbria' itself is a Celtic term, similar to 'Cymru', which is the Welsh term for Wales.

Only South Cumbria was mentioned in the Domesday Book in 1086, while Scotland and England held most of Cumbria at different times in the 11th and 12th centuries. Even when Cumbria was finally ceded to England, the Scots frequently raided. Much of the land was granted to monasteries, who developed large-scale sheep farms, or 'granges'. Carlisle, which had been a military site from Roman times, had its defences continually strengthened during centuries of conflict between England and Scotland.

Following the dissolution of the monasteries in the 16th century, estates were sold, and a number of independent farms were established, whose owners were known as 'statesmen'. The Lake District was quarried and mined for minerals, while the lowland fringes were much more heavily exploited. Booming industrial towns and ports were created, chiefly Barrow-in-Furness, and a network of railways began to be constructed during the 19th century.

The writings of the 'Lake Poets', about the beginning of the 19th century, raised awareness of the Lake District among travellers. William Wordsworth, Samuel Taylor Coleridge, Robert Southey and Thomas De Quincey romanticised the area in their writings. This paved the way for tourism, increased road transport, more railways, the building of hotels and lodging houses, and the Lake District as we know it began to take shape. Wordsworth was an outspoken critic of such developments.

By 1951 the area was already famous as a walking destination, and the Lake District National Park was established: see page 18. The county of Cumbria was created in 1974, merging the old counties of Cumberland, Westmorland and North Lancashire, and the Cumbria Way was launched at the same time.

2·4 Habitats and wildlife

Great Gable from near Esk Hause

When humans first entered the Lake District, the valleys were tangled with dense woodland and lake margins were choked with vegetation. Tree cover was extensive, mainly oakwoods, thinning at higher altitudes to leave rocky summits protruding. Today's habitats have been influenced by thousands of years of human occupation, and most notably by centuries of intensive sheep-grazing, leaving the fells looking barren. Below we describe the area under four headings: waterside, woodland, moorland and fell.

Waterside

There are two major lakes on the Cumbria Way – Coniston Water and Derwent Water. Both contain trout and perch, while Coniston Water is notable for char and Derwent Water also contains roach. Both lakes are busy with visitors in summer, which keeps most wildlife distant, although birds such as swans and mallards are attracted by people feeding them. Bird watchers find the lakes more rewarding in winter, when they attract a greater variety of ducks, geese and other fowl.

Watch rivers carefully to spot dippers, which use their wings to stay underwater while feeding. Herons are seen infrequently, but stand out because of their size and slow-motion, low-level flight.

Shelduck

Although the Cumbria Way is some distance from the coast, gulls are seen around Ulverston and Carlisle, and lonely moorland pools will occasionally attract raucous groups of black-headed gulls, or waders such as curlew, with its distinctive 'bubbling' call.

Curlew

Ospreys had been absent from the Lake District for 150 years until a pair nested near Keswick and fished in Bassenthwaite Lake in 2001, and raised a chick. Since that time ospreys have re-appeared annually and have bred successfully. Osprey viewing areas are established annually near Keswick and details can be checked at ***www.ospreywatch.co.uk***.

Woodland

Only small remnants of the original oakwoods that once covered the Lake District remain, clinging to rocky slopes where they regenerate without too much interference from sheep. There are many colonies of juniper, mostly struggling, but surviving because of re-planting and controlled grazing.

Although there are many mixed woodlands, most are secondary plantations, having been harvested for timber in the past, or managed as coppices for the production of charcoal. Modern plantations, mostly dating from the 1900s, are generally dense coniferous forests, featuring non-native trees. The poet Wordsworth had a particular dislike of larch trees when they were introduced.

Spreading oak tree

Cumbria is one of England's last outposts for red squirrels, which have largely been displaced elsewhere by grey squirrels. Polecats barely cling to existence and are rarely seen. Deer are common, but generally seen only at dawn and dusk when they venture to graze alongside woods, where they can quickly retreat if disturbed.

Red squirrel

Moorland

The most extensive moorlands on the Cumbria Way are the ones 'Back o' Skiddaw', featuring swathes of heather that are flushed purple in the middle of summer. This area is particularly important for ground-nesting birds, such as red grouse, with its distinctive 'ge-back ge-back' call. Ground nesters also include stonechat, lapwing, short-eared owl and merlin. The months of April and May are crucial for nesting and rearing young: disturbance caused by people walking off-path or, worse still, allowing dogs to run free, can have fatal results.

Some moorland areas are wet and boggy. Permanently waterlogged ground may be covered in sponge-like sphagnum moss, or it may sprout clumps of rushes. Look out for sticky insectivorous plants, such as butterwort, or more rarely, sundew. In a couple of places, such as near Beacon Tarn or at the head of Derwent Water, the aromatic shrub called bog myrtle grows profusely. It is used by some as protection against midges.

Red grouse

Bell heather

Fell

Open fells in the Lake District have been developed over many centuries as rough grazing for sheep, particularly Herdwicks. As a result of grazing, they are generally covered in short grass, heather and bilberry. Flowers tend to be small and inconspicuous, but some species, such as foxgloves, are tall and colourful. Invasive bracken often dominates the lower slopes, and trees only survive if they can grow out of reach of sheep. The most notable trees to grow in rocky clefts on the fells are rowans, also known as mountain ash. Thorny gorse bushes grow on many fellsides, covered in bright yellow flowers that smell similar to coconut.

Rocky areas look lifeless, but are usually crusted with blotches of lichen. Cracks in the rock and gaps on rocky scree often sprout clumps of parsley fern. The poet Southey claimed it was 'the most beautiful of all our wild plants, resembling the richest point lace in its fine filaments and exquisite indentations'. It cannot tolerate lime, or competition with other plants, so it is confined to the most rugged central parts of the Lake District.

Ravens roost high in the fells and are year-round residents, seeking carrion wherever they can find it. They are the biggest members of the crow family, and show off incredible flying skills, even flying upside-down at times, and make a deep 'cronk-cronk' call. Other big birds noticed on the fells include buzzards, and very rarely golden eagles.

There are foxes on the fells, and five packs of foxhounds are kennelled in the Lake District, with the nearest pack to the Cumbria Way being at Coniston. Huntsmen, who are mostly fell-farmers, follow the dogs on foot, rather than horseback, because of the rugged terrain. The most famous huntsman, immortalised in song, was John Peel (1776-1854) who is buried at Caldbeck. It became illegal to hunt foxes with dogs in 2005, so most 'hunts' now follow a scent trail to keep the dogs exercised.

Upper: Parsley fern
Inset: Gorse flowers
Lower: Fox in woodland

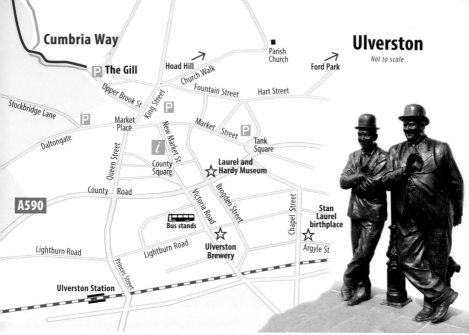

Laurel and Hardy statue, Coronation Hall

Ulverston is a historic market town with a population of 11,500. It was mentioned in the Domesday Book in 1086 and its market charter was granted by King Edward I in 1280. Its canal opened in 1796 and meant that ships no longer had to beach on Morecambe Bay at low tide. It was the shortest, straightest, widest and deepest canal in the country and brought prosperity. Ulverston filled with warehouses and its population doubled.

Situated on the north-west edge of Morecambe Bay, travellers to Ulverston used to have to brave quicksands, deep river channels and fast-moving tides. In the mid-19th century, all that changed with the arrival of the railways following construction of long viaducts over the treacherous tidal channels of the Rivers Kent and Leven.

The town is dominated by the monument on Hoad Hill, a replica of the Eddystone Lighthouse. Built in 1850 and restored in 2010, it celebrates the career of Sir John Barrow, born in Ulverston in 1764, who moved to London and became second secretary to the Admiralty from 1804 to 1845. Hoad Hill (133 m/ 435 ft) is an easy walk from Ulverston, best approached via Church Walk, the Parish Church and Ford Park: see map above.

Another son of Ulverston was Arthur Stanley Jefferson (1890-1965), who became famous as comedian Stan Laurel. He returned to Ulverston in 1947 with his partner Oliver Hardy, and their statues outside the Coronation Hall were unveiled in 2009. The Laurel and Hardy Museum lies behind the Roxy Cinema: see page 70 for details.

Ulverston is a dedicated Festival Town with a variety of events throughout the year, including a Walking Festival around April/May. The Visitor Information Point is in the Market Hall in the town centre: see map above and page 70 for a link to useful websites.

3·1 Ulverston to Coniston

Distance	15·7 miles 25·2 km
Terrain	field paths and low fell paths, occasionally faint; well-wooded lakeshore walking; good tracks; short road-walking sections
Grade	mostly fairly gentle, but with a few short, steep ascents and descents
Food and drink	Ulverston (wide choice), Old Hall Farm (weekend snacks), Lowick Bridge and Torver (pubs off-route), Coniston (wide choice)
Summary	gentle field paths and country lanes, followed by low and occasionally boggy fells, then a well-wooded lakeshore walk

0   5·5   6·4   3·8   15·7

Ulverston 8·8 **Gawthwaite**   10·3   **Sunny Bank** 6·1 **Coniston**

- To reach the start of the Cumbria Way from your accommodation, or from bus or train station, use the map on page 24. At the far end of The Gill is the 'Cumbria Waymarker', a metal spire that encloses a display of the route's geology: see page 14.

- Just beyond it, a plaque marks the start of the route which leaves along a broad tarmac path beside a beck, keeping left at a fork. There are iron railings on the left, and a steep slope of bushes on the right. The valley becomes well-wooded with a solitary house, and the official CW turns left across a stone bridge.

- You could instead divert to avoid Old Hall Farm – useful if you hesitate to pass through a field with cattle, especially if you have a dog with you. Simply continue straight ahead, later leaving the woods to cross a small field to a road. Turn left along the road, and left again for Old Hall Farm. Turn right through a small gate between two houses to rejoin the CW.

- After the stone bridge, the CW climbs a steep walled path, reaching a kissing-gate and road. Stop just short of the road, and squeeze through a very narrow gap-stile on the right, marked by a fingerpost and Cumbria Way signs. On a clear day, you may glimpse the distant peak of Coniston Old Man framed in the valley.

Cumbria Waymarker, The Gill

Narrow gap-stile, just before road

- Keep a stone wall on your left through fields, then follow a track flanked by wire fences. Turn right to go between buildings at Old Hall Farm as marked. As soon as you pass the farmhouse, turn left through a small gate.

- Follow a very short riverside path and cross a step-stile on the left. Walk across a muddy field, aiming for a gap-stile that may still be marked by a large red circular plastic lid. Climb beside a wood where bluebells grow in early summer.

- Cross a step-stile and climb across a field, near a small stream. A fine garden lies to the right, overlooked by the large house of Boretree Stile. Go through two little gates to the left of the house and climb beside the stream in a small wooded valley.

- Cross a beck by footbridge and a wall by step-stile. Walk straight across a sloping field and cross a wall by ladder-stile. Climb through a slight valley, to follow a path between gorse bushes and brambles, then cross a wall by step-stile.

- Walk across a field and cross a stone wall by step-stile to reach the farm of Higher Lath. Enjoy views from Morecambe Bay and Ulverston to the Lakeland Fells.

Beyond Hoad Hill to Morecambe Bay

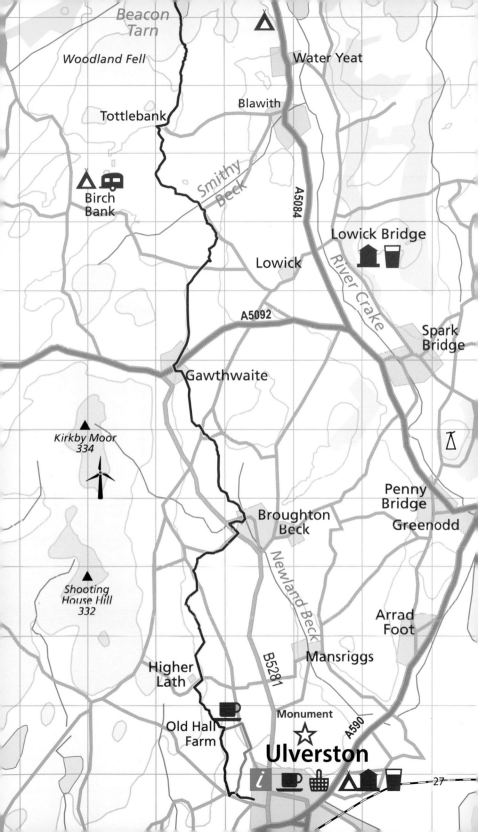

Beacon
Tarn

Woodland Fell

Water Yeat

Tottlebank

Blawith

Birch
Bank

Smithy Beck

A5084

Lowick Bridge

Lowick

River Crake

A5092

Spark
Bridge

Gawthwaite

Kirkby Moor
334

Penny
Bridge

Greenodd

Broughton
Beck

Newland Beck

Shooting
House Hill
332

Arrad
Foot

Mansriggs

B5281

Higher
Lath

A590

Old Hall
Farm

Monument

Ulverston

27

- Turn right and walk 200 m down a steep road, turning left as signposted through a gate.

- Walk straight across two fields, then turn right to walk diagonally down through two more fields and cross a step-stile over a fence.

- Cross a little stream and climb stone steps, then walk across a field to a farm called Stony Crag. Go through two gates just to the left of the farmhouse, then spot a marker on a telegraph pole on the right showing the path leading onwards.

- Go through a gate and follow a stone wall that reaches only halfway across a field. At the end of the wall, go through a little gate on the right, cross a small beck and turn left to walk upstream to the farm of Hollowmire. Go through a gate, turn right through the concrete farmyard, and follow the access road as it climbs gently.

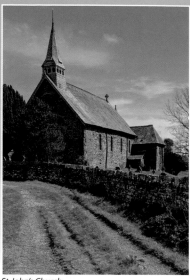

St John's Church

- Turn left at a 'T' junction, signed 'Cumbria Way'. Follow the undulating road until, just after a telegraph pole, you reach a left-hand bend. Ignore a short track that drops to the right, instead looking behind nearby trees to spot a gate with yellow marker pointing right: enter a field.

- Walk across the field and through a gate, then aim for St John's Church: see photo above. Keep left of it, and go through gates to reach a road where you turn right. Reach a T-junction with the B5281 road, where there is a bench.

- Turn left as signed for Broughton, then turn right down into the hamlet of Broughton Beck, where many houses include 'mill' within their names. Keep left and follow a cul-de-sac to its end, and continue ahead after the tarmac ends. Cross a beck and follow a track to another beck, but do not cross it.

- Turn left through a gate and follow a track past a building. Go through another gate and keep to the left side of a field. Pass through a further gate and turn right at the end of the field, crossing a step-stile.

Near Higher Lath Farm

Coniston Old Man

Wetherlam

Beacon Fell

- Walk across a field and cross a stone-slabbed footbridge. Turn left upstream and cross a step-stile. Follow a stone wall and cross a step-stile, then follow a line of trees onwards. Another wall leads to a curious step-stile, climbing one wall, but coming down another.
- Turn right to follow a track up to a road, then turn left along the road, at the foot of a rugged slope. Go through a gate and pass the farm of Knapperthaw, then turn right at a road junction.
- Before approaching another road junction, look for a short-cut left along a short grassy track to a telegraph pole and CW signpost.
- Cross a cattle grid between stone pillars and follow a farm track down through a gateway into a wood. Look out for a boulder engraved 'Keldray Farm', turn left (signed 'Footpath' at ground level) up a path on a wooded slope. Do not cross the first step-stile you see, but climb a short way up the steep wooded slope and cross another step-stile over a fence at the top.
- Turn right along the edge of the wood. Cross a step-stile (or keep left to avoid it), then keep left of a power line to spot a little gate in a wall on the other side of a sloping field. Walk beside a wall across the next field to the far side. Turn left up a broad path flanked by stone walls.
- Go through a gate and follow an access road between houses to reach the A5092 road in the hamlet of Gawthwaite. Cross the road to a grassed triangle to reach a road junction beyond, here entering the Lake District National Park.
- Follow a small grey slate marked 'Cumbria Way' along a road on the right. Go down past some houses and turn left uphill at the first road junction (where the sharp-eyed may spot a tiny timber CW sign on the wall). There are views back to Ulverston's Hoad Hill, as well as right across the gentle Crake Valley; to the left there's an old slate quarry.
- Go through a gate on a road surface that deteriorates, while views stretch ahead to the Coniston Fells. Catch a glimpse of Coniston Water ahead while climbing to a height of 180 m (590 ft). Go through another gate, down into a dip, and through a further gate. Turn right as signposted, still on the old road, down through a gate beside trees. Stay on tarmac, down through more gates, bending around a house at High Stennerley.

Gawthwaite

- Follow the road down past patchy woodland and grassy slopes to a junction. Turn right downhill, then left after 50 m at the first gate to enter a field as signed. (If instead you continue down the road, you could reach the Red Lion pub [with accommodation] at Lowick Bridge: turn right at one road junction and left at another.)
- Follow a narrow path straight ahead rising gently across a wet slope, later crossing a stone step-stile beside a gate. Stop near a water trough, and look right to spot a boulder bearing a waymark disc. It is important to locate this boulder before you continue walking.
- Walk down through the field towards its bottom corner, where there is an inconspicuous stone step-stile. Cross this carefully (it's awkward on the far side) to reach a narrow road.
- Turn left to follow the road, which winds through woods, rises and falls, and reaches a junction. Turn left as marked 'Kiln Bank only', down into a dip then up to the farm of Kiln Bank.
- Turn right at the very last building and climb from one gate to another. Bear left across a slope to follow what becomes a fine grassy track.
- Keep right at a junction, still climbing, and level out gradually. (Keeping left at the junction leads to a farm campsite at Birch Bank, 1·3 km away.) Follow the track down through a gate, reaching wet and muddy ground.
- The track climbs to a road, where you turn left as if going to the farm of Tottlebank. At the top of the road, however, turn right up a grassy path. This is broad and clear, even when the bracken on either side is growing tall.
- The path rises and falls, reaching a stone wall. Keep left to find a gate marked 'Cumbria Way'. Go through it and follow a wall ahead, well to the left of farm buildings at Cockenskell. Go down through another gate and down a short path on a steep, wooded slope.

Tottlebank

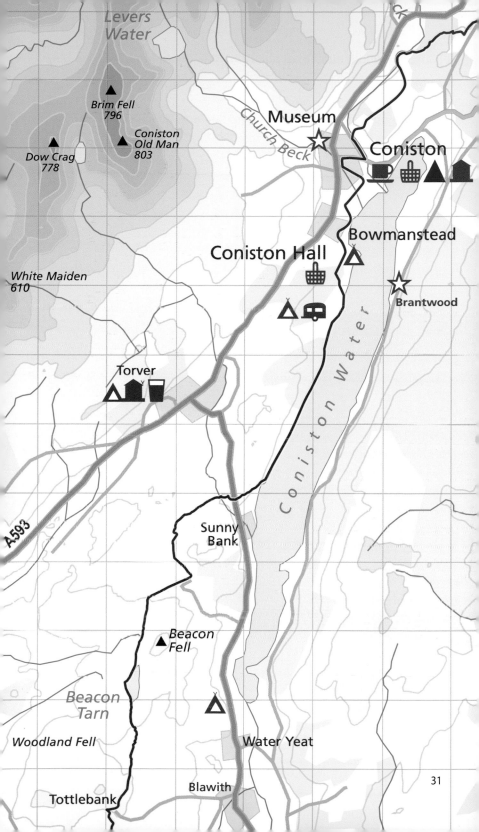

Levers Water

Brim Fell
796

Coniston
Old Man
803

Dow Crag
778

Church Beck

Museum

Coniston

Coniston Hall

Bowmanstead

White Maiden
610

Brantwood

Coniston Water

Torver

A593

Sunny
Bank

Beacon
Fell

Beacon
Tarn

Woodland Fell

Water Yeat

Tottlebank

Blawith

31

Lakeshore path, Coniston Water

- Turn left to cross a little stone-arched bridge over a beck. Go through a gate, follow a path uphill and keep left at a junction. Follow the clearest path uphill, crossing a gap to see Beacon Tarn, with the Coniston Fells rising far beyond. Beacon Fell is the rugged hill ahead, slightly to your right. Bog myrtle grows in damp areas.

- Turn left to walk along the shore of the tarn, crossing wet and boggy areas. The path is firmer later, crossing a gap at around 190 m (625 ft) beside Beacon Fell. Continue ahead, descending with bog to the left in places, and a bouldery slope to the right.

- About 1 km after the end of Beacon Tarn, follow the clearest path to a road, roughly north-east. After crossing Black Beck, you reach the road at a sharp bend, with a signpost pointing back to Cockenskell.

- Turn left up the road for about 100 m to a signpost pointing off left. Follow the clearest path which goes down, up and then down again, roughly parallel to a power line. (The other path rejoins the clearest path later.)

- Cross a small beck, then cross a larger one (Mere Beck), walking towards and almost reaching a little unnamed tarn. (Beyond the tarn, a path links with farm tracks leading off-route to Torver which has pubs, accommodation and a campsite.)

- The Way avoids the tarn by turning right at an unmarked path junction about 200 m after Mere Beck. Head down through its valley, passing twisted juniper bushes.

- The path leads to a footbridge across Torver Beck and its cascades. Walk up through a kissing-gate to the A5084 road. (Buses run from here to Ulverston and Coniston, except at weekends. To allow a bus to stop safely, turn right for 300 m down to Sunny Bank.)

- Cross the road to a small car park and a sign reading 'Coniston via lake shore'. Walk up a track, round to the left, and down through a gate with a view of Coniston Water. The path descends to the lake, reaching a jetty for the Coniston Launch: see page 70.

- The lakeshore path is quite rugged, with lots of ups and downs on a slope of mixed woodland. It is hard to measure progress, but the path later goes through a small gate in a stone wall, then heads right among tall conifers.

- Pass the end of another stone wall, and another jetty for the Coniston Launch, and cross a footbridge. The path runs broad and easy through woods and is also used by cyclists. Pass a gate, boathouse and a further jetty, where there is access to a nearby campsite.

The Campbells and Bluebird
Sir Malcolm Campbell set various world speed records, his last being on Coniston Water in August 1939 (142 mph). His son Donald broke his father's records on both land and water. In 1964 his unique double was to set new records for both – 403 mph (land) and 276 mph (water). He died in January 1967 while trying to exceed 300 mph, when his craft 'Bluebird' flipped over, disintegrated and sank. The wreckage wasn't discovered until 2000, and Campbell's body was retrieved only in 2001. Visit the Ruskin Museum for the full story and to see 'Bluebird'.

- Follow the lakeshore path until it drifts from the shore to follow an access road through another campsite. Pass the 16th century Coniston Hall, which has thick walls and massive chimneys. (There is a small campsite shop here.)

- The CW avoids Coniston Sailing Club, following a road between two barns, then turns right along a gravel track. This runs through gates and winds from field to field, all the way to some retail units on Lake Road on the outskirts of Coniston.

- Turn left to follow Lake Road to a crossroads with the main road (A593). Turn right to follow the road to a bridge and road junction in the centre of Coniston.

Coniston is a large village (population over 1000), strongly associated with the writer and critic John Ruskin. Ruskin lived at Brantwood, about 5 km away, and his house is well worth a visit. Failing Brantwood, make time for Coniston's own Ruskin Museum, which has an excellent collection including geology and mining: see page 70 for both museums. Coniston Water and nearby features were amalgamated with Windermere to form the backdrop for Arthur Ransome's Swallows and Amazons books. The village has a fair choice of accommodation, refreshments and shops, and its Tourist Information Centre is in a car park behind St Andrew's Church. There are daily buses to Hawkshead and Ambleside and, except at weekends, to Ulverston.

Coniston Hall

Distance	**11·6 miles 18·7 km**
Terrain	woodland paths and tracks; gentle riverside and lakeside path; good valley paths and tracks from village to village and farm to farm
Grade	fairly gradual ascents and descents, occasionally short and steep; mostly level when following rivers in the dales
Food and drink	Tarn Hows (snacks), High Park (teas), Elterwater Park (teas) , Skelwith Bridge (pub and café off-route), Elterwater (pub), Chapel Stile (pub and café), New Dungeon Ghyll (pub), Old Dungeon Ghyll (pub)
Summary	gentle low hills, with woods, fields, and fine fell views; opportunities to break at tea gardens and pubs, while heading to the heart of the Lake District

15·7		6·5		5·1	27·3
Coniston		**10·5**	**Skelwith Bridge**	**8·2**	**Old Dungeon Ghyll**

- Start from the bridge in the centre of Coniston. Follow the road signed for Hawkshead, past The Crown and almost to Yewdale Beck. Don't cross the bridge, but turn left up Shepherds Bridge Lane, signed for Skelwith and Ambleside, and follow it as far as Coniston Primary School.

- Turn right over a bridge signed as a 'public footpath'. Turn left along a narrow path and go through a kissing-gate. The path continues up through another kissing-gate beside a castle-like folly. This was built as a dog-house on the Monk Coniston estate in the late 19th century. Nowadays it houses information boards, seats and shelter.

- Follow the path uphill beside a fence and go through a gate. The path is flanked by gorse bushes as it climbs, levelling out at a kissing-gate. Go through a wood and soon leave through another gate. Descend a grassy slope with a stone wall on the right, enjoying fine views around Yewdale.

- Follow the track downhill, but watch on the left for a large oak tree with marker posts nearby. Leave the track on an untrodden section that soon leads to a gate beyond the oak tree.

- Walk down through a field to reach another gate, turning left along a track. This runs upstream beside Yewdale Beck, reaching a stone-arched bridge. Don't cross the bridge, but keep straight on through a kissing-gate on its right, signed 'Tarn Hows'.

Tarn Hows Cottage

- Walk around a field and go through a kissing-gate into a wood, to follow an obvious path beside a stream. The path climbs through the wood, and drops to cross a small footbridge. Further uphill, exit the wood through gates and pass the attractive Tarn Hows Cottage.

> **i** **Tarn Hows**
> This iconic Lake District beauty spot is actually an entirely man-made scene. A marshy hollow known as The Tarns was dammed on the orders of James Garth Marshall. He was a Yorkshire mill owner, said to be rather harsh with his work-force. He bought the Monk Coniston estate and used the water from Tarn Hows to power a sawmill in Yewdale. Marshall also had the trees planted around the tarn. The area was purchased by Beatrix Potter and was donated to the National Trust.

- Turn right at the fingerpost and pass through a gate to walk up the cottage's access track, which after hairpin bends soon meet a one-way road. Turn left up the road, enjoying fine views of fells from Coniston Old Man and Wetherlam to the Langdale Pikes and Fairfield. Cross a cattle grid and pass a car park with toilets, where you may also see a snack van and a National Trust recruitment vehicle.

- Turn left at a National Trust notice for Tarn Hows and walk down either of two paths leading to a small dam at the outflow. Go through a gate to cross the dam and follow an undulating path beside the well-wooded shore. The path starts beside the shore, later veering away, with numbered marker posts.

- About 50 m after post number 7, turn left at a junction signed 'Arnside and Langdales'. The path is rugged, leading out of the woods to a kissing-gate and a broad track.

- Turn left to follow the rough undulating track, which is flanked by walls and in places worn to bare rock. It offers a good view of Wetherlam to the left, and later meets a narrow road.

- Turn left down to a crossroads on the A593 road at Oxen Fell. Cross over and turn right to walk parallel to the road, through a wood and fenced off section of field.

Tarn Hows

High Park, Little Langdale

- After 300 m the fenced off section ends: don't return to the road here, but turn left along an unmarked path to walk to a junction of minor roads. Follow the undulating road signed for High Park and Hallgarth for 1 km.

- Turn right down its access road to approach the farm at High Park, where a tea garden may be operating. The rugged Lingmoor Fell rises beyond.

- Turn right in front of the farm through a kissing-gate signed 'Public Bridleway'. Cross a field and go through another kissing-gate, then follow the path to a further kissing-gate and enter an oakwood.

- Almost immediately there is a fork. Keep right for the CW, or detour left (an extra 100 m) to visit the waterfall of Colwith Force (recommended after heavy rain). The detour rejoins the CW where it exits the wood to reach a road near Colwith Bridge.

Leaving Tarn Hows for Oxen Fell

- Turn right along the road, then left to cross a stone step-stile with a little gate on top. After a short field path, climb 50 wooden steps up a steep, wooded slope. Cross a step-stile into a field, follow the path up towards buildings and cross a private access road.

- Follow a narrow, enclosed path, crossing two step-stiles to reach more buildings at Elterwater Park Country Guest House. Walk between farm buildings, which have B&B facilities; a tea barn and tea garden sometimes operate here.

- Go through a gate and follow a track downhill, then go through another gate and cross a dip. Climb and keep right of Park House, walking up its access track until it levels out.

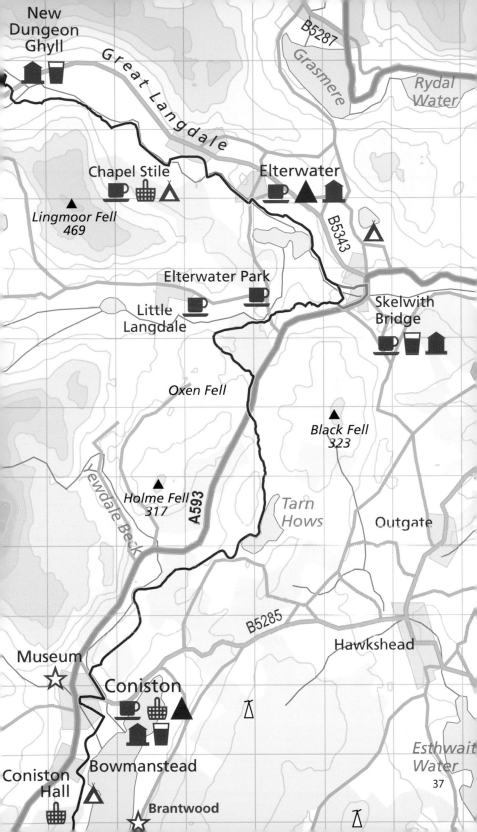

New
Dungeon
Ghyll

B5287

Grasmere

*Rydal
Water*

Great Langdale

Chapel Stile

Elterwater

B5343

*Lingmoor Fell
469*

Elterwater Park

Little
Langdale

Skelwith
Bridge

Oxen Fell

*Black Fell
323*

Yewdale Beck

Holme Fell
317

A593

*Tarn
Hows*

Outgate

B5285

Hawkshead

Museum

Coniston

*Esthwaite
Water*

37

Coniston
Hall

Bowmanstead

Brantwood

- At a junction, turn left to follow the path down through a kissing-gate into a wood. Later, a path junction is reached. Keep left for the CW, or right to visit Skelwith Bridge (see later). Left leads through woods and across a metal footbridge. At that point, a slight detour right leads to the waterfall of Skelwith Force in 50 m, otherwise turn left.

- For Skelwith Bridge, turn right and follow a path to the A593 road. Turn left along the road, later crossing a bridge; the Skelwith Bridge Hotel lies ahead. Turn left to a café and continue past a former slateworks. Pass Skelwith Force and rejoin the CW at a footbridge where you go straight ahead. This detour adds 400 m to the route.

- Go through a large gate to leave the woods, avoiding the kissing-gate alongside – a very tight squeeze. A clear path runs through a meadow beside the River Brathay, later reaching the shore of Elterwater, with the Langdale Pikes rising beyond.

Between Elterwater Park and Park House

- Follow the path through a gate into woods, leaving the lake views behind. Later, the path runs beside the wood, then beside the river to reach Elterwater, which has accommodation, a pub, café, toilets and a daily bus services linking Langdale with Ambleside.

- Cross the bridge over Great Langdale Beck. Turn right to follow a cul-de-sac uphill, flanked by large boulders from nearby slate quarries. After walking 400 m and before reaching the quarries, turn right downhill to follow a riverside path below quarry spoil. Keep to the footpath as it veers away from the river, then cross a footbridge and go through a gate to reach a road.

- Turn left to pass Wainwrights' Inn on the edge of the village of Chapel Stile. (Head just along the road for toilets, shop and café.) Turn left up a stony track signed 'Baysbrown Campsite avoiding road', following a narrow road behind the primary school grounds.

- Turn left along the road, then bear right (signed 'footpath'), keeping right of buildings at Thrang Garth. Walk down a walled path, through a little gate, and turn left along a track, crossing a bridge over Great Langdale Beck to reach the Baysbrown Campsite.

- Stay on the track running parallel to the beck, through gates from field to field, drifting from the riverside later. The track veers left and runs up to the farm of Oak Howe. (To reach Robinson Place Farm, a B&B 900 m distant, turn right, and cross a bridge over the beck. Walk up to the B5343 road and turn left, then right up the farm access road.)

Heading for the Old Dungeon Ghyll Hotel

- To continue the CW, walk past the barn behind Oak Howe and turn right along an undulating path flanked by low stone walls, going through a gate. Rise again across the foot of Lingmoor Fell, with views of the Langdale Pikes. The path is rugged, with several becks to cross, one by means of a huge stone slab footbridge.

- Descend to pass through a gate at a sheepfold, then descend steeply on a reconstructed stone path. After it levels out, go through a gate to reach a footbridge and farm at Side House.

- Follow a track away from the farm, crossing a bridge over the beck to reach the B5343. Turn left along the road and almost immediately right to enter the Stickle Ghyll Car Park. There are two options: turn left to short-cut through fields to the Old Dungeon Ghyll Hotel (see foot of page) or turn right to stay on the CW, walking through the car park towards toilets and the Sticklebarn Tavern, with New Dungeon Ghyll Hotel beyond.

- At the top end of the car park, turn left up a path and follow it through a gate, past a bird-feeding station. Notices explain which birds might be seen. Follow the path uphill, past a National Trust plaque 'Stickle Ghyll'. Soon afterwards, fork left up a more rugged path, with increasingly fine views as you climb.

- Go through a gate in a wall at the top of the slope. Keep left at a fork, where another path climbs to Pike o' Stickle. Cross a footbridge over a beck with small waterfalls and pass a small barn and farmhouse before reaching the buildings of Old Dungeon Ghyll.

- Turn left down through a gate to Old Dungeon Ghyll for hotel accommodation, food, drink, toilets, nearby campsite (with shop) and buses to Ambleside. The CW keeps right to continue through Mickleden.

- The short-cut leaves the car park and passes the farm of Rossett. Cross a footbridge and roughly follow a path upstream through fields. Reach another car park and head straight for the buildings at Old Dungeon Ghyll to rejoin the CW behind the hotel.

Distance	7·3 miles (11·7 km)
Terrain	steep and rugged fell paths; occasionally boggy valley paths; good riverside tracks and paths
Grade	steep and arduous ascent and descent, requiring careful navigation in mist, gradually giving way to easier valley walking
Food and drink	Stonethwaite (pub off-route), Rosthwaite (pubs and café)
Summary	easy valley path, then steep, rugged fell-walking, followed by a remote valley path leading to farmland and fields

27·3		2·5		4·8		34·6
Old Dungeon Ghyll	4·0		Stake Pass	7·7		Rosthwaite

- From behind Old Dungeon Ghyll Hotel, keep left through a gate. Follow a stony track past a National Trust sign for Mickleden. The track becomes enclosed by stone walls as far as a gate and sheepfold.

- Uphill to the right you'll see Pike o' Stickle and its screes, where stone axes were once fashioned. Stake Pass (your target) is the lowest gap in view, and Rossett Pike rises above the head of the valley. Bowfell lies to the left, followed by The Band and Pike o' Blisco. Lingmoor Fell lies down the valley behind you.

- Keep following the obvious stony path upstream, passing little pools, then cross a wooden footbridge overlooking a circular stone sheepfold. Note a stone on the right, carved with 'Stake Pass' and 'Esk Hause'. Just beyond, turn right at a cairn and pass a stone engraved 'Cumbria Way'.

Approaching Stake Pass

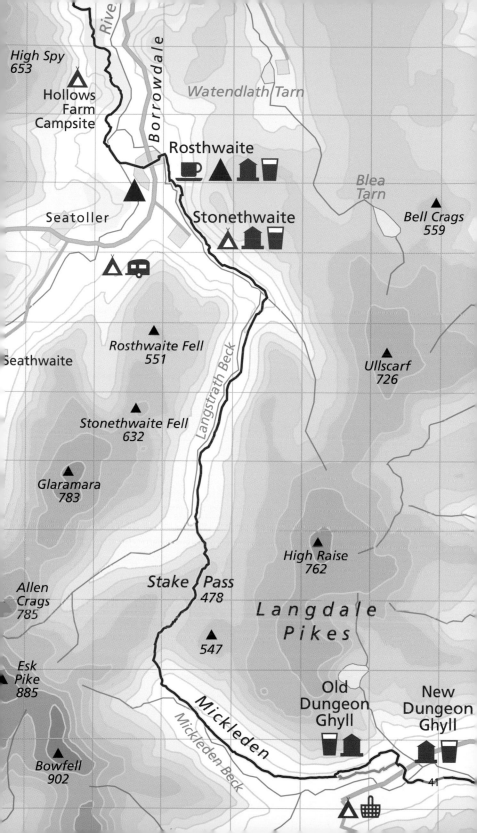

High Spy
653

Hollows
Farm
Campsite

River

Borrowdale

Watendlath Tarn

Rosthwaite

Seatoller

Stonethwaite

*Blea
Tarn*

Bell Crags
559

Seathwaite

Rosthwaite Fell
551

Langstrath Beck

Ullscarf
726

Stonethwaite Fell
632

Glaramara
783

High Raise
762

Allen
Crags
785

Stake Pass
478

L a n g d a l e
P i k e s

547

Esk
Pike
885

Mickleden

Mickleden Beck

Old
Dungeon
Ghyll

New
Dungeon
Ghyll

Bowfell
902

41

- A constructed path twists and climbs steeply to the left of Stake Gill, always clearly defined but tough going. The route becomes more rugged and veers north-east across Stake Gill: by now you have ascended to 400 m, with another 78 m of altitude still to gain. (Stake Pass takes its name from the wooden stakes that used to mark it.)

Cairn on top of Stake Pass

- Continue to gain height, but at an easier gradient in Langdale Combe, which has occasional stepping stones over wet and boggy patches. Ignore a path on the right (for the Langdale Pikes) and another on the left (for Rossett Pike).

- Keep straight ahead to a cairn on Stake Pass, near a rock carved with an arrow. At 478 m (1568 ft), this is one of the highest points on the CW and on a clear day you'll see fine views, with Skiddaw far ahead directly to the north.

- A narrow gravel path descends gently at first, then winds round lots of hairpin bends on a steeper slope. Further down the path is more rugged, passing waterfalls on Stake Beck. Cross a waymarked footbridge over the beck, but keep ahead and don't be tempted off-route towards another footbridge to the left.

- The path continues downstream, roughly parallel to Langstrath Beck and valley, crossing grassy slopes dotted with boulders, boggy patches and a few trees. Eventually, cross a ladder-stile over a stone wall at the foot of Sergeant's Crag. The path has a wire fence to the left at first, then a stone wall, and is still quite rugged in places.

Graphite and pencils

At nearby Seathwaite in Borrowdale, Britain's only pure deposits of graphite were mined from the mid-16th to mid-19th centuries. Graphite had many uses, from cannonball moulds to lubricants. Locally, it was used to mark sheep, but was messy to handle. However, strips of graphite were sheathed in wood to keep hands clean, and a pencil-making industry was founded. This moved from cottage enterprise to a purpose-built factory in Keswick in 1832, but manufacture recently moved to Workington. The CW passes Keswick's Pencil Museum: see pages 47 and 70.

Downstream beside Langstrath Beck

View back over Sergeant's Crag (right) and Eagle Crag (centre)

- After passing under a huge spreading larch tree, go through a small gate in a stone wall. Continue downstream and avoid a footbridge. There are more trees and another small gate, then a stretch runs close to the beck, which has many boulders and cascades.

- Cross a footbridge over Grains Gill. Go through a gate and turn left along another path, now shared with Wainwright's famous Coast to Coast route.

- The path runs downstream, but also rises through a gate. Descend gently and go through another gate where a campsite can be seen across Stonethwaite Beck.

- Cross a footbridge over a little beck and follow either a walled path or a parallel grassy path, then go through another gate. A walled track leads straight ahead through a further gate. (A bridge on the left leads off-route directly to Stonethwaite in 200 m, where a pub offers food, drink and accommodation.)

- Follow the track straight ahead through another gate, and later round a bend where the river also bends sharply.

- Reach a road and turn left to follow it over a bridge over Stonethwaite Beck to meet the B5289 road just outside Rosthwaite. Turn left to walk straight ahead into the village, or turn left, then quickly right, to continue along the CW. Rosthwaite offers accommodation, pubs, food and drink and regular buses to Keswick.

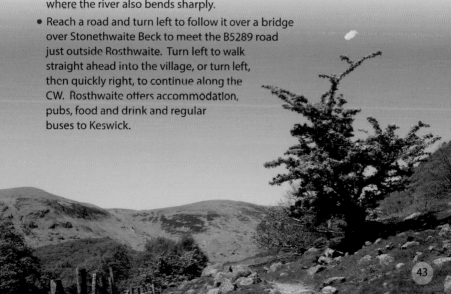

3·4 Rosthwaite to Keswick

Distance	8·2 miles (13·2 km)
Terrain	good riverside tracks and paths; well-wooded lakeshore paths; ending in a busy town
Grade	easy valley and lakeshore walking with only a few short ascents and descents
Food and drink	Grange's (café off-route, pub), Lingholm (café off-route), Nichol End (café off-route), Portinscale (pubs), Keswick (wide choice)
Summary	easy walking through woods and fields, with charming lake scenery and views of surrounding fells, ending in a busy tourist town

34·6			4·5			3·7		42·8
Rosthwaite			**7·2**	**High Brandelhow**		**6·0**		**Keswick**

- Leave Rosthwaite by following the narrow road opposite the pillarbox, signed Yew Tree Farm. Pass the Village Hall and toilets, walk through the farmyard (or visit the Flock-In tearoom) and then follow a walled track between fields.

- Follow the River Derwent, cross a stone-arched bridge and continue downstream on its west bank. Go through the rightmost of two gates. The track then veers away from the river into mixed woodland below Castle Crag (mainly oak and birch).

- Follow the path as it undulates and then descends back to the riverside. After more undulations, it goes through a gate and descends to cross two footbridges over streams. Reach a barrier gate where a campsite lies up to the left.

- Bear right to follow the track onwards through woods to a road and fingerpost. (The village of Grange with its cafés and toilets lies 600 m off-route to the right.) The Way turns left up the road to Hollows Farm.

- Follow a track that runs ahead, beyond the farm and to its right, across a wooden bridge. Fork left to follow another track up through a gate, and stay on the track heading down a little, then go up it to the corner of a wood.

Bridge over River Derwent

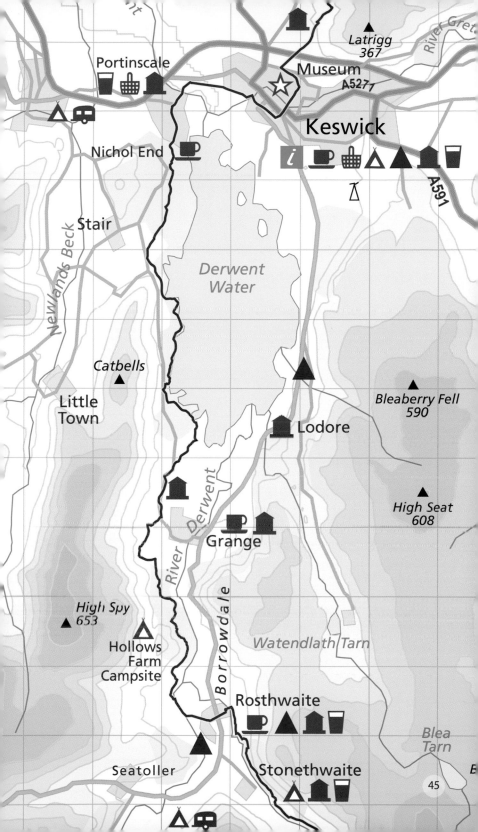

Latrigg
367

Museum
A5271

Portinscale

Keswick

Nichol End

Stair

Newlands Beck

Derwent Water

Catbells

Bleaberry Fell
590

Little
Town

Lodore

River Derwent

High Seat
608

Grange

High Spy
653

Borrowdale

Watendlath Tarn

Hollows
Farm
Campsite

Rosthwaite

Blea
Tarn

Seatoller

45

Stonethwaite

A591

River Greta

- Go through a gate on the right and turn right then left, down through a field dotted with trees, overlooking the village of Grange. Exit by a gate onto a road opposite the Borrowdale Gates Hotel. (Turning right would quickly take you to Grange.)
- Turn left along the road. After 400 m, it crosses Ellers Beck: on its far side turn right through a gate signed for Lodore.
- Follow the track downstream and cross a little footbridge. Keep to the path through two more gates, then immediately turn left. There are views of the southern end of Derwent Water, with Skiddaw (left) and Blencathra (right) in view beyond.
- Aim towards the lake and turn left along a gravel path and raised duckboards. At The Warren, turn right along a narrow road and follow a path close to the lake shore. Bear right through an unmarked gate to pass the foot of a mining spoil heap. Walk for over 1 km through mixed woodland, passing jetties at High Brandelhow and Low Brandelhow. (Both jetties are served by the Keswick Launch: see page 70.)
- Leave the woods and enter a field where there are two paths. The CW turns left beside the field and goes through a gate. Follow the broad path through more gates and rise to a road. Turn right along the road to pass an outdoor centre at Hawse End. Bear right along the road at the end of its car park.
- Ignore the jetty access, and avoid also the private road after it, also down to the right: instead take a fenced path whose gate is just past the private road junction, signed 'Portinscale 1·5 miles'.

Duckboard path near Derwent Water

Nichol End Marina

- Descend through the woods, cross a footbridge and continue through a field. Go through a gate, re-entering woods, the path rising and falling past big oak and beech trees.
- Later you cross a road to the Lingholm estate, a possible detour for its café and walled garden with Beatrix Potter connections. Afterwards continue as signed for Portinscale and Keswick, but fork left almost at once, beside a wall.
- Climb steadily on a path flanked by oak, beech and rhododendron, then descend and turn right along a road. (Another right turn leads off-route to Nichol End Marine, named after St Nicholas, with a café and another jetty for the Keswick Launch.)
- Walk on the pavement to follow the road past Derwent Bank, and cross the road where the pavement switches sides, passing Derwent Lodge and Derwent Marina.
- Go down the road to a junction in Portinscale. Turn right along the cul-de-sac, past the Derwentwater Hotel, and cross a fine suspension footbridge over the River Derwent.
- Follow a short riverside path ahead and turn right at its end, signed for Keswick, along a broad, fenced path between fields. Go through kissing-gates and eventually turn left along a road, then right along a busy main road into Keswick, passing a sign to the famous Pencil Museum, home to the world's biggest pencil: see page 70.
- Walk straight ahead into a pedestrianised area to finish at the Moot Hall, a fine building which houses the Tourist Information Centre: see page 70. Note that throughout Keswick, CW markers are fixed to signs above eye level. Regular buses run to Carlisle, Borrowdale, Workington, Penrith, Ambleside, Windermere, Kendal and Lancaster, with less frequent buses to Caldbeck.

Keswick

Keswick is a market town (population about 5000) and a popular base for fell walkers and climbers – the self-styled 'Adventure Capital of the Lake District'. It has a wide choice of accommodation and plenty of pubs, restaurants, cafés and shops (including good outdoor gear) and other facilities: Keswick hosts a number of festivals, including the Keswick Mountain Festival. Its Theatre by the Lake features a range of classic and modern plays and performances.

St Herbert, a lifelong friend of St Cuthbert, had a hermitage on St Herbert's Island in Derwent Water. According to legend, both saints died at the same time in the year 687, and the island became a pilgrimage site. Pilgrimages were used as an opportunity to trade, and Keswick received its market charter from Edward I in 1276. These days, the annual 'Keswick Convention' features a summer season of bible study.

In the 16th century, graphite was worked in nearby Borrowdale: see panel on page 42. The world's first pencils were produced on a small scale, then a factory was opened in Keswick in 1832. The story is told in Keswick's excellent Pencil Museum, which you passed on your way in from the west.

Novelist Hugh Walpole set his Herries Chronicles series of books in and around Keswick, drawing inspiration from many locations and houses. The series follows four generations of a family over a period of 200 years.

Keswick Museum & Art Gallery collection includes enormous stone xylophones, or lithophones. The stones were collected and fashioned over several years and despite their considerable weight, have been used for concerts around Britain and Europe. See page 70 for details of Keswick's visitor attractions and TIC.

Approaching Keswick: Skiddaw (left) and Skiddaw Little Man (right)

3·5a Keswick to Caldbeck (main)

Distance	**15 miles (24·1 km)**
Terrain	good tracks and paths into remote fells; rugged moorlands on the ascent of the highest point on the route, where careful navigation is required; good paths and tracks further downhill; road-walking near Caldbeck
Grade	steep climb followed by ascending paths, narrow and rocky in parts; remote moorlands with faint paths; careful navigation needed on both ascent and descent of High Pike
Food and drink	Caldbeck (pub and café)
Summary	a steep track, gentler path and a rocky path lead into a remote area, with some riverside paths, but the broad slopes of High Pike are exposed and require careful navigation

42·8   5·6   8·1   1·3   57·8

Keswick   9·0   **Skiddaw House**   13·0   **Nether Row**   2·1   **Caldbeck**

- Leave the Moot Hall and turn a nearby corner at The Royal Oak at Keswick, onto Station Street. Continue straight across Victoria Street at a crossroads and go down Station Road, across a bridge over River Derwent, and past Fitz Park and the Keswick Museum & Art Gallery.

- Turn left up a tarmac path and cycleway which passes the forme52r Keswick Leisure Pool, keeping right of the building. Pass a car park to reach a mini-roundabout where you turn left up leafy Brundholme Road.

- Ignore a junction where another road turns right, but step right to continue along the roadside path, keeping beside the road to pass houses at Briar Rigg. Within 150 m turn right along a gravel track signed 'Skiddaw 4 miles'. This is Spooney Green Lane, which climbs and crosses a bridge over the busy A66 road.

Looking back to Keswick from Latrigg Woods

- There is a dip in the track, then it climbs past Spooney Green House and goes through a gate into Latrigg Woods, with information boards on the left. The track climbs steeply through mixed woods, with glimpses through the trees on the left to the towering Skiddaw Fells.

- Stay on the clearest track uphill, avoiding all paths and tracks to the right, and go through a gate. Later, the ascent becomes gentler, with wider-ranging views beyond Keswick and Derwent Water to Whinlatter, Grasmoor, Newlands and beyond.

- Pass a notice-board for Gale Ghyll Woods and a forest plantation on the left. Afterwards, ignore a path sharp right signed for Latrigg Summit, instead keeping straight ahead to follow the track across an open slope. Go through a gate to reach a road, and turn right to go to and through a road-end car park.

- Go through a gate and turn left, following a Public Bridleway signed for Skiddaw, parallel to a wall and fence that rises gently through another gate. Once through the gate, the path forks: turn right to follow a narrow path. (The broad path to the left climbs Skiddaw – one of the highest fells in England.)

- Follow the path down past a few larch trees and ford a beck, then walk up a broad, stony path. The steep slopes of Lonscale Fell are covered in grass, bracken and rushes. A fine panorama stretches from Blencathra to Whinlatter via the Helvellyn range, central fells and north-western fells.

- The broad path swings left into the valley of the Glenderaterra Beck, through a gate. The path abruptly becomes narrow, hacked from slate and following rocky terraces across a steep slope of heather and bilberry. Looking ahead through the valley, the conical form of Great Calva is seen. Afterwards, the path becomes easier again.

On Lonscale Fell, heading towards Great Calva

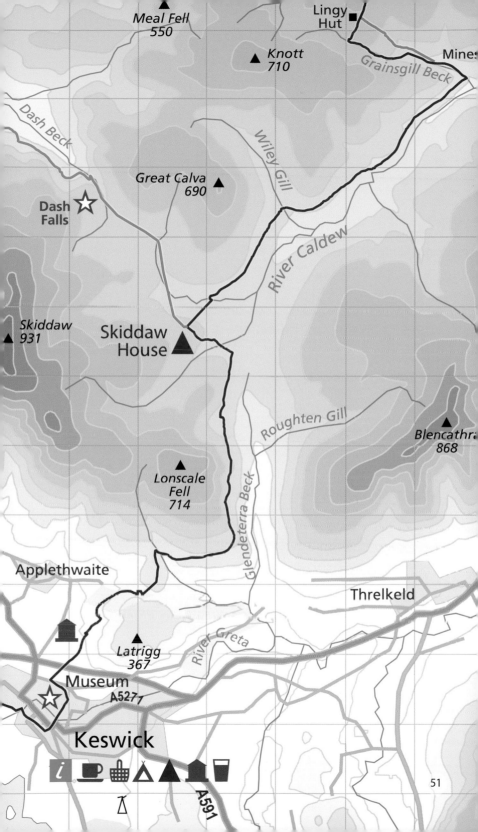

Meal Fell
550

Lingy
Hut

Knott
710

Mines

Grainsgill Beck

Dash Beck

Wiley Gill

Great Calva
690

River Caldew

Dash
Falls

Skiddaw
931

Skiddaw
House

Roughten Gill

Blencathra
868

Lonscale
Fell
714

Glenderterra Beck

Applethwaite

Threlkeld

Museum

Latrigg
367

River Greta

A5271

Keswick

A591

Skiddaw House

- Ignore another path rising from across the valley, and go straight ahead on gentler slopes. Go straight ahead through a gate in a fence to follow a path across heather moorland, soon sighting Skiddaw House Youth Hostel ahead, surrounded by stone walls and larch trees.

- Cross a footbridge over Salehow Beck and walk up to the far end of the hostel's stone wall, where the route divides. The main route turns right, heading north-east down a narrow path, whilst the alternative route goes ahead north-west along the access track away from Skiddaw House.

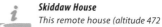

Skiddaw House

This remote house (altitude 472 m) was built before 1830 to accommodate gamekeepers and shepherds in separate dwellings, as well as to shelter grouse-shooting parties. The building has been altered many times. The last shepherd to live here was Pearson Dalton, who arrived in 1922, supposedly only for a month, but stayed until 1969. Since the 1990s the building has operated as the highest hostel in England, normally with an option to camp. Note that food and drink are available only to those who have booked to stay overnight: see **www.skiddawhouse.co.uk**.

- If cloud is obscuring the summit of Great Calva (the fell north of Skiddaw House), visibility will be poor on High Pike and you are advised to take the alternative route from here to Nether Row, described on pages 58-60. In fair weather, take the main route, described below, to enjoy outstanding views from the highest point of the Way.

- Just beyond Skiddaw House, turn right beside a tumbled stone wall and descend across soft ground. Cross a footbridge over the infant River Caldew, follow a stony path uphill, then level out on softer ground.

- The path runs gently downhill and passes left of a circular stone sheepfold. You'll pass another sheepfold where a footbridge crosses Wiley Gill, about 3 km after Skiddaw House. The distant fell with summit cairn ahead to your right is Carrock Fell.

- Go through a gate in a fence and follow a stony path gently uphill, then a gritty path gently downhill. Two more stone sheepfolds lie to the right, and the second incorporates a ruined hut. Continue along a grassy path and pass below a solitary Scots pine. Ford Burdell Gill to reach the end of a stony track.

- Ignore a grassy track climbing left, and bear right on the stony track parallel to the River Caldew to ford Wet Swine Gill. Later, ignore another track on the right that descends to the river past a barrier gate. Go ahead to cross a bridge over Grainsgill Beck. From the bridge, look upstream to spot Lingy Hut perched on the skyline – an important landmark on a stretch that is almost devoid of waymarks or signs.

- Swing right briefly along a road, then turn sharp left up a narrow road (a Public Bridleway) signed for Miller Moss, past a barrier gate to reach old mining spoil heaps. (A notice explains that mineral picking requires a permit.) In case of need for an escape route, follow the road down the valley for 3 km to Mosedale and hope for a B&B and/or taxi pickup.

- The CW route now follows Grainsgill Beck upstream, unless you opt for the alternative shown on page 55. The next kilometre is steep, awkward and wet with no proper path: you may need to use hands as well as feet in places and you will find it very slow going. A beck called Arm o' Grain is forded halfway up Grainsgill Beck.

Grainsgill Beck, with Lingy Hut on the horizon

- When you reach level boggy ground at the top of Grainsgill Beck, or as soon as you can see Lingy Hut, turn or bear right to head for the hut at around 600 m (1970 ft). The hut offers basic shelter in one of the most remote parts of the entire Way, and its ends carry the only CW waymarks for miles: you may wish to sign its visitor book.

Lingy Hut, before it was timber-clad

High Pike

At 658 m/2158 ft, this is the highest point on the CW, with exceptional views in clear weather. Looking back into the Lake District, there are glimpses beyond Skiddaw and Blencathra to the Scafells and Eastern Fells. Parts of the Yorkshire Dales and North Pennines are in view across the Vale of Eden, with the Cheviot Hills far beyond Tynedale. The Southern Uplands of Scotland stretch from the Liddesdale Hills to the Lowther Hills and Galloway Hills, with Criffel rising prominently across the Solway Firth.

Memorial bench, with Bowscale Fell distant

- Follow the clear undulating track that leads past Lingy Hut. From the brow of a rise, you'll finally see your goal: the rounded fell of High Pike marked by a summit cairn.

- Look ahead to the boggy dip in the moorland from which two grassy paths head uphill off the main track. Neither is waymarked, but take your pick to reach the broad summit of High Pike, with its cairn, trig point, viewfinder and stone memorial bench.

Views from High Pike, loosely based on the summit location finder

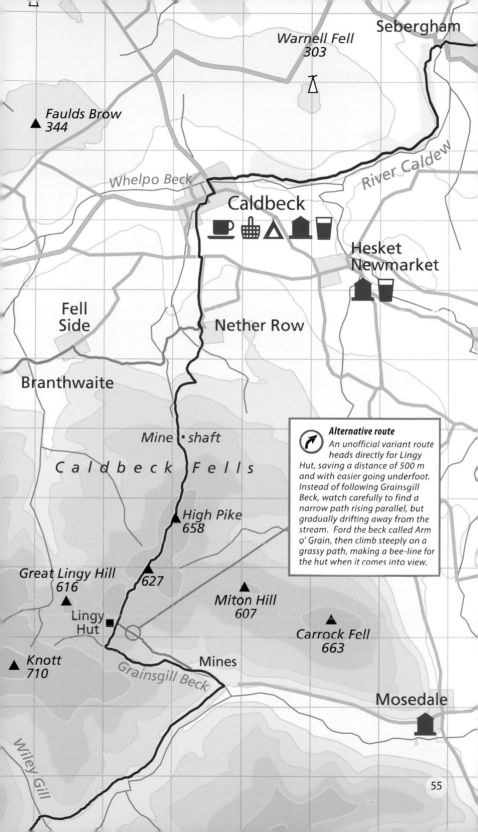

Sebergham

Warnell Fell
303

Faulds Brow
344

Whelpo Beck

River Caldew

Caldbeck

Hesket
Newmarket

Fell
Side

Nether Row

Branthwaite

Mine · shaft

C a l d b e c k   F e l l s

High Pike
658

Great Lingy Hill
616

627

Miton Hill
607

Carrock Fell
663

Lingy
Hut

Knott
710

Grainsgill Beck

Mines

Mosedale

Wiley Gill

Alternative route

An unofficial variant route heads directly for Lingy Hut, saving a distance of 500 m and with easier going underfoot. Instead of following Grainsgill Beck, watch carefully to find a narrow path rising parallel, but gradually drifting away from the stream. Ford the beck called Arm o' Grain, then climb steeply on a grassy path, making a bee-line for the hut when it comes into view.

- Take great care on the descent from High Pike, especially if visibility is poor, as you cross featureless ground. Set off roughly northwards, and align the direction of the red 'Caldbeck' arrow in our diagram against the viewfinder itself. Walk 100 m to a pile of stones (the remains of a building), keeping just to the right of it.

- A grassy path veers slightly right (north-north-east) along a crest: follow this down a short steep slope, but only for 100 m until it levels out. It is very important then to turn left along a lesser grassy path to continue the descent. Two ill-defined paths head left: choose the most trodden down one to descend the featureless slope, and stick to it.

- Watch the ground ahead and if after 800 m you spot a fenced-off mining shaft to the right, you are on course: see main photograph below. You should also see a small, bare hump of mining spoil, at the far left and in close-up. Turn right, gently up a grassy track, then turn left down another grassy track.

- Next, cross a stony track near a larger bare area of mining spoil at Potts Gill Mine, and continue straight ahead down a clear track. The track drifts to the right, around another spoil heap, later bending left and right, through a gate and passing between buildings at Clay Bottom Farm.

- Walk down the farm road, straight over a complicated junction (where the CW alternative joins from the left) to the collection of farms and buildings known as Nether Row.

- From Nether Row, follow a tarmac road straight ahead (north). When the road bends left, a right turn along a track could be used to reach a camping barn, 1·5 km off-route at Hudscales, but its sign (on a beech tree) may be overgrown.

Descent from High Pike past a fenced mineshaft

Bare hump of mining spoil (close-up)

Priests Mill, Caldbeck

- The road continues for 1 km down between fields. At a crossroads, go straight ahead along an overgrown former road flanked by hedges. Ignore the first footpath that turns right through a gate and walk on a further 75 m to the next turning, with CW marker. Very soon turn left over a step-stile into a field, watching for yellow marker arrows.

- Cross the field and go through a gate into another field, then look left of the telegraph pole for a step-stile to cross a farm track. Go through a kissing-gate and walk beside a hedge, down through a field and past a telegraph pole through a gate.

- Go down a tunnel-like woodland path and cross a beck using a stone-arch bridge. If it's unduly wet and muddy underfoot you can exit to the lane to reach a road junction.

- Turn left at the end of the path, then turn right to join the steep road (B5299) down to the village of Caldbeck to reach a road junction beside the Oddfellows Arms.

- To continue the CW, turn left along the road signed 'Wigton 7, Carlisle 13'. Caldbeck has a little accommodation, including a campsite and also a shop.

Oddfellows Arms, Caldbeck

3·5b Skiddaw House to Caldbeck (alternative)

Distance	12·5 miles (20·1 km)
Terrain	good tracks past remote fells; undulating field and woodland paths, followed by road-walking at Orthwaite; paths, tracks and roads around moorland fringes; road-walking near Caldbeck
Grade	remote moorlands with good tracks; undulating field and woodland paths; road walking; undulating paths and tracks on moorland fringes
Food and drink	Bassenthwaite (pub off-route), Caldbeck (pub and café)
Summary	although a greater distance than the main Way, this alternative is not more tiring and it is easier to navigate

```
0·0          5·1                      6·1                  1·3      12·5
O─────────────────────O──────────────────────O─────────────O
Skiddaw House  8·2    Orthwaite        9·8    Nether Row  2·1  Caldbeck
```

- Follow the access track away from Skiddaw House, down to a ford and footbridge on the infant River Caldew, then up a heather moorland slope. Cross a dip where Dead Beck flows, then rise and level out with a view ahead of a distant hill called Binsey.

- The track is bendy as it descends, and the top part of Dash Falls, or Whitewater Dash, is seen. Further down the track, more of the waterfall can be seen, but most is hidden by trees. Go through a gate and cross a bridge over a beck at the foot of rugged Bakestall.

- Walk down to a tarmac road and turn left up it, then follow it down through gates and fields, eventually reaching a road near Peter House. Cross the road to find a step-stile and signpost beside gates.

- Don't follow a clear track through a field, but veer left as marked by a blue arrow. Aim for the furthest corner of the field and go through a gate.

- A four-way signpost indicates a right turn for the CW. (Bassenthwaite is straight ahead, off-route.) Walk in a straight line beside four fields, from gate to gate, with the farm of High Close off to the left. A final gate stands beside a wood: go through and descend into the wood, crossing a step-stile and a footbridge over Halls Beck.

- Turn right, cross a road and climb a steep, forested slope. Cross a ladder-stile at the top and turn right along a nearby track, fording a shallow beck.

- Rise to a gate and step-stile, but don't follow the track ahead. Instead, turn left over a grassy, pathless hill. (Alternatively, for a clear feature, follow the fence and hedge to the left.)

Winding descent from 'Back o' Skiddaw'

Ireby

Aughertree Fell
321 ▲

Uldale

Over
Water

Dale Gill

Orthwaite

Longlands Beck

Meal Fell ▲
550

Bassenthwaite

A597

Dash Beck

Dash ☆
Falls

Great Calva ▲
690

Barkbeth Gill

Skiddaw ▲
931

Skiddaw ▲
House

- Reach a gate, ladder-stile and a four-way signpost on the far side of the hill. Cross the stile as signed for Orthwaite, then cross a grassy hill with a view of Little Tarn down to the right and Skiddaw rising beyond. Descend steeply and cross a wooden bridge over a sluggish beck.

- Walk ahead, then turn left over a step-stile, and continue uphill. Keep left of a gate and go through a higher gate. Continue through a field until a marker arrow points right through a gate. Aim for a solitary house flanked by two other groups of buildings. A stone step-stile leads to a road beside Orthwaite Cottage.

- Turn left and follow the road for 2·5 km as it winds and climbs, with a view of Over Water down to the left. Keep straight ahead at a crossroads, signed for Caldbeck. (Turn left off-route for Uldale.) Look left to spot Chapel House Reservoir, then climb steeply, later levelling out with Longlands Fell rising to the right.

- Go down the road to cross Longlands Beck, then before climbing to houses at Longlands, turn right through a gate marked 'Uldale Commons'. Follow a track uphill, sometimes grassy or stony, with views back towards Skiddaw and Over Water.

- The track later bends right, drops to ford Charleton Gill, rises a little, then descends gently on a moorland slope. Walk straight ahead down a tarmac road, crossing a bridge with white railings. Turn right at a road junction at Greenhead and cross a stone-arched bridge.

- Follow the road for 2·5 km through farmland, including a short, steep descent past farm buildings at Branthwaite.

- Cross a bridge and climb steeply past an old school, reaching the hamlet of Fell Side. Follow the road past all the buildings before turning right along a track to reach a gate.

- Climb gently on parallel concrete strips across a grassy slope and approach a farm at Little Fell Side. Don't drop down to the buildings, but follow a stone wall straight ahead, then take a path across a wet, grassy slope to a farm at Potts Ghyll.

- Cross a beck before turning left through a little gate. Walk down to the farm access road and turn right to follow it, crossing cattle grids and another beck; then walk gently uphill to Nether Row.

- Turn left along a tarmac road, to be joined by the main Way from the right. Resume directions from the top of page 57 to reach Caldbeck.

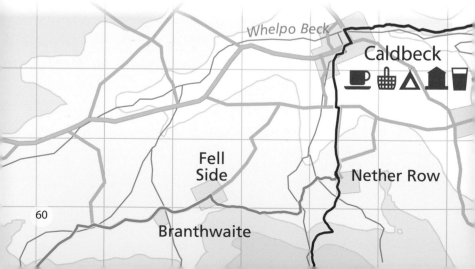

3·6 Caldbeck to Carlisle

Distance	**15·5 miles 25·0 km**
Terrain	mostly riverside tracks and paths, with woods and fields; occasional short road-walks; follows a tarmac riverside cycleway from Dalston to Carlisle
Grade	some short, gentle ascents and descents, but mostly level and easy
Food and drink	Bridge End (pub), Dalston (pubs and cafés), Cummersdale (pub off-route), Carlisle (wide choice)
Summary	a long but fairly easy walk, mostly following the River Caldew through gentle farmland to Dalston, ending with rapid progress along a cycleway to the border city of Carlisle

57·8 — 10·0 — 5·5 — 73·3
Caldbeck — 16·2 — Dalston — 8·8 — Carlisle

- Leave Caldbeck by following the road signed for Wigton, crossing a bridge over Cald Beck, here leaving the Lake District National Park. Turn right (Public Bridleway for Sebergham Bridge) following a road roughly parallel to the river.

- Go ahead through a gate and continue along a track, then step to the right of a small sewage works.

- Go through a gate and follow a broad gravel track climbing from the river on a wooded slope with fine views of High Pike and Carrock Fell. Walk straight along a broad, undulating path, and continue up a narrower path to pass through a small gate.

- Walk across a grassy slope, with woods below and thorny gorse bushes above. Halfway across the field, ignore a trod path that bears down to a step-stile.

- Near the field end, another trod path runs gradually down towards the wood and a large gate, but the CW stays higher. Go through a smaller gate to the left, on a Public Bridleway.

- Walk across another large field, apparently blocked ahead by a wood, but stay high and look left for another small gate at the far left corner of the field, with an old CW marker.

- Follow a gravel path through the wood, which rises towards a gate. Don't go through the gate, but bear right down the narrow path, descending steeply through woods to the riverside. Walk the well-wooded path downstream.

St Kentigern's Church, Caldbeck

Looking back towards High Pike

- Go through a gate to leave the wood, passing a boulder and keeping to the left side of a field. Go through another gate and follow a track onwards, passing fields, woods and wild rhubarb, to reach buildings, a final gate and a road. Turn right to cross the River Caldew by the stone-arched Sebergham Bridge.

- Turn left, signed 'Public Bridleway Sebergham Church', through a small gate. The path swings right and climbs to another small gate.

- Pass a large red brick house and follow a road straight ahead for 500 m to St Mary's Church.

- Turn left through gates opposite the church signed as a Public Bridleway for Bell Bridge, following a clear track. Approach stone gate pillars and white gates near Sebergham Hall, but step to the right through another gate, and follow a track that links with another track.

- The track descends to a road, where you turn left to cross Bell Bridge. After the old bridge was destroyed during Storm Desmond in 2015, the new bridge opened in 2017. Turn right as signed through a gap in its parapet, and descend steep, slippery steps with care.

- For the next 2½ miles (4 km) walk downstream on the west bank of the River Caldew. Starting down the right side of the next field, simply keep close to the river and you'll find gates, stiles and little footbridges over streams wherever you need them.

- About halfway through this section, you pass Bog Bridge on your right, and about 750 m later, go through a gated stretch of mixed woodland beside the river. Shortly after, you'll see Rose Castle, and soon reach a road with the fine three-arched Rose Bridge.

River Caldew from Sebergham Bridge

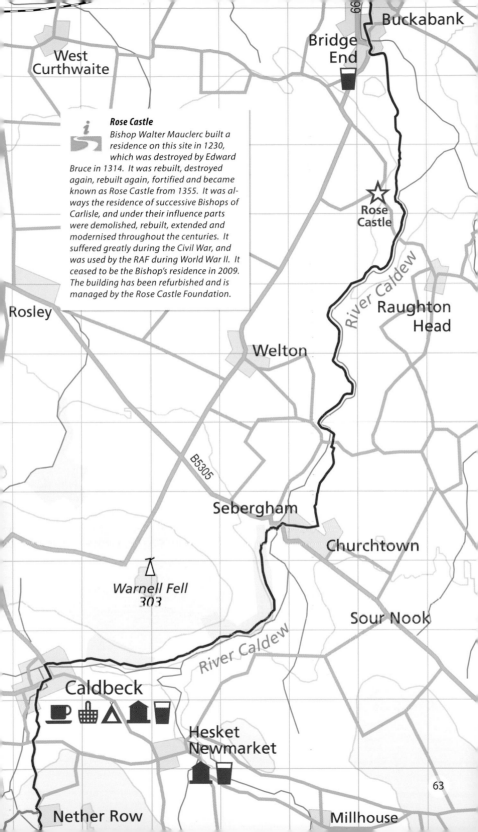

Buckabank

Bridge
End

West
Curthwaite

i **Rose Castle**
Bishop Walter Mauclerc built a
residence on this site in 1230,
which was destroyed by Edward
Bruce in 1314. It was rebuilt, destroyed
again, rebuilt again, fortified and became
known as Rose Castle from 1355. It was always the residence of successive Bishops of
Carlisle, and under their influence parts
were demolished, rebuilt, extended and
modernised throughout the centuries. It
suffered greatly during the Civil War, and
was used by the RAF during World War II. It
ceased to be the Bishop's residence in 2009.
The building has been refurbished and is
managed by the Rose Castle Foundation.

Rose
Castle

River Caldew

Raughton
Head

Rosley

Welton

B5305

Sebergham

Churchtown

Warnell Fell
303

Sour Nook

River Caldew

Caldbeck

Hesket
Newmarket

Nether Row

Millhouse

Rose Castle

- Cross the road, using stone steps and kissing-gates, to continue along the riverside path signed for Holm Hill. About 500 m after Rose Bridge, the river bends sharply right and the way ahead is blocked by a wood. Turn left away from the river on an unmarked trod path to a footbridge incorporating a small gate.

- Walk up through a field to a kissing-gate, then follow a faint path to a metal kissing-gate. Turn left along a track 'Public Bridleway Holm Hill' flanked by tall oak trees and cross the access road to Lime House School.

- Go through a kissing-gate, crossing a field northward past trees to reach a large gate near a house. Turn left to follow its access road uphill, then turn right down a narrow tarmac road, almost to another house.

- Go through a gate on the right, at a large cedar tree, to follow a field track gently down, then straight uphill. Follow the track up through a gate into a large field and keep following it down through another gate.

- Turn left on a path overlooking a weir, and exit the field through a gate to follow a road past houses. Turn right at a junction to walk down the busy B5299 road to the Bridge End Inn on a road bend.

Field track en route to Bridge End

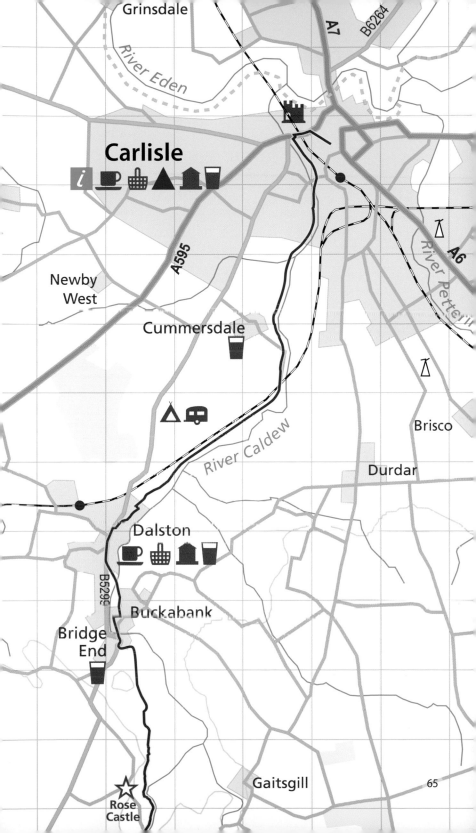

Grinsdale

River Eden

A7

B6264

Carlisle

Newby
West

A595

Cummersdale

River Caldew

Brisco

Durdar

Dalston

B5299

Buckabank

Bridge
End

Gaitsgill

A6

River Petteril

Rose
Castle

65

Celebration of Dalston's Black Reds football team

- Turn right, signed for Durdar, to cross Hawksdale Bridge over the River Caldew. Go straight ahead, keeping left along the road called Riverside. Turn right at the end of it and follow a road across a 'weak bridge'.

- Turn left at the fingerpost along a road beside a mill race to pass through the substantial red sandstone buildings of a former mill. Continue ahead to another stretch of mill race, then turn left and cross the White Bridge over the River Caldew.

- Take the road across a green space to join the busy B5299. Turn right to walk along the main road through Dalston, your last refreshment opportunity before Carlisle. It has various shops including the well-known bakery Crumbs, also pubs and regular daily buses to Carlisle.

- Follow the main road as far as St Michael's Primary School and turn right as signed for the Caldew Cycleway, whose tarmac you now follow for nearly all 8 km into Carlisle. Signs ask cyclists to stay on the right, and walkers to keep left.

- There are numbered posts along the path: at number 4 (near the large Nestlé factory) a short riverside path can be followed instead of the cycleway.

- After 2 km, the cycleway runs close beside the railway, at first sandwiched between it and the river, and in one stretch marked with a flood risk sign. The river then drifts away to the right for a while, returning within 900 m.

- Shortly both cycleway and River Caldew pass beneath a railway bridge and a gate soon leads onto a road. Follow it straight ahead, passing a footbridge to reach a factory near Cummersdale.

- Approach close to the factory gates to find a narrow path between factory fence and river. When you reach steps and a ramp uphill, bear right of the ramp to follow a wooded riverside path leading into a grassy area called Cummersdale Holmes.

- The path stays close to the river, while the cycleway rises further away for a while. (In very wet weather, follow the cycleway.) Follow the clearest path until you see fencing ahead: bear up the rightmost of two paths up to gates at a housing development.
- Turn right along a broad path between the River Caldew and housing (a former mill). Pass a large weir and keep beside the river, passing a footbridge and playing fields.
- Pass another footbridge and continue straight ahead along McIlmoyle Way, through a new housing development, where a flood barrier wall screens the river. There's a mixture of new and old housing, as well as factories.
- Reach Elm Street floodgate. From here, the official CW takes an indirect mile-long route around central Carlisle to the Tourist Information Centre (TIC): to complete this, turn left through the floodgate to pass under a road bridge.

- Alternatively, if you are running late for a train, or need to go straight to your accommodation, you could leave the Way and reach the city centre within 300 m. Walk up the cobbled street to steps and turn right over Nelson Bridge. Bear left up Victoria Viaduct to reach a junction. From here, the TIC is about 200 m to your left and Citadel Station about 200 m to your right.

- The main Way passes a supermarket and crosses a footbridge mounted on an old railway bridge over the River Caldew. At the end of the cycleway, turn left up a road to reach Castle Way. Turn right along the pavement and keep Tullie House Museum on your right as you turn into Castle Street. CW markers are above eye level.
- Continue ahead, passing Carlisle Cathedral on your right, to enter a large pedestrianised area centred on the Market Cross. The TIC is inside the Old Town Hall, and you may wish to leave comments in the book that it holds for CW walkers. **Congratulations on completing the Cumbria Way.**

Path beside the River Caldew near Cummersdale

Carlisle

Old Town Hall, Carlisle

Carlisle developed as a a garrison town. It is Cumbria's only city, with a population exceeding 108,000. There was probably a fortified settlement on this site before the Romans arrived in 79 AD. The Roman fort was called Luguvalium, and was later an integral part of Hadrian's Wall, which was constructed in 122 AD. Following the departure of the Romans, legends of King Arthur feature around Carlisle and further afield. Carlisle Castle dates from 1092, and has been considerably rebuilt and extended.

Known as the 'Border City', Carlisle saw conflict during the Dark Ages and Middle Ages, especially during centuries of strife between Scotland and England. Edward I, the 'Hammer of the Scots', journeyed from Carlisle to nearby Burgh Marsh in 1307, where with his dying breath he cursed Scotland.

Carlisle expanded greatly during the Industrial Revolution. It had a short-lived canal, an enduring railway network, and plenty of mills and factories, handling everything from biscuits and textiles to engineering. Pedestrianised streets are crammed full of shops, pubs, cafés and restaurants, all within easy walking distance.

Carlisle Castle

The city centre is remarkably compact. Carlisle Cathedral dates from 1122, when it was an Augustinian church. Although the monastery it served was dissolved in 1536, some of the original buildings remain nearby, including its Fratry which houses a splendid café. Parts of the city walls still stand, and The Citadel has impressive drum towers.

The Tullie House Museum, between the Cathedral and Castle, tells the full story of Carlisle and has an excellent section on Roman history. See page 70 for more on Carlisle's visitor attractions, museum and TIC.

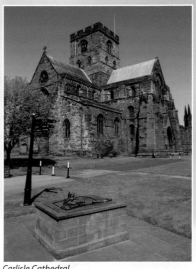

Carlisle Cathedral

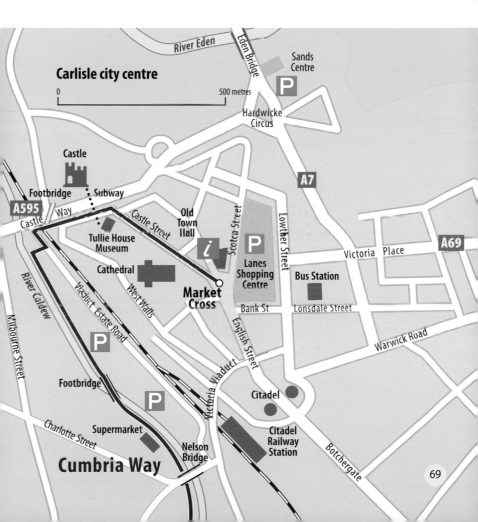

4 Reference

Cumbria Way

The Cumbria Way was created in the mid 1970s by local Ramblers Association members, and first described by Ramblers stalwart John Trevelyan. The route is not an official National Trail. The Lake District Area of the Ramblers Association promotes the route and allows walkers to report problems and check for advice on temporary closures. Visit this page within The Ramblers website:

bit.ly/cumbriaway

Lake District websites

Cumbria Tourism is the main contact for all kinds of tourist information in the area:

www.visitlakedistrict.com

Lake District National Park Authority

www.lakedistrict.gov.uk

National Trust

www.nationaltrust.org.uk

Websites about towns along the Way

There is plenty of interest in the main towns along the Cumbria Way, but to explore them properly means taking extra time. Please visit our website page

www.rucsacs.com/books/cbr

and follow its Route Links for good websites that cover accommodation, facilities, visitor attractions and events in Ulverston, Coniston, Keswick and Carlisle.

Public transport

Ulverston and Carlisle have good rail links, while long-distance coach services offer good budget approaches. Local bus services in the Lake District are mostly operated by Stagecoach: see page 7 for a map. Always consult up-to-date time-tables before setting off.

National Rail Enquiries:
www.nationalrail.co.uk
National Express:
www.nationalexpress.com
Citylink:
www.citylink.co.uk
Traveline:
0871 200 2233 (charges apply)
www.traveline.info
Coniston Launch, Coniston Water:
01768 775 753
www.conistonlaunch.co.uk
Keswick Launch, Derwent Water:
01768 772 263
www.keswick-launch.co.uk

Wildlife

Cumbria Wildlife Trust:
www.cumbriawildlifetrust.org.uk
Osprey Watch:
www.ospreywatch.co.uk
Natural England:
bit.ly/natural-england

Museums

Laurel & Hardy Museum, Ulverston:
01229 582 292
www.laurel-and-hardy.co.uk
Ruskin Museum, Coniston:
01539 441 164
www.ruskinmuseum.com
Brantwood Museum, near Coniston:
01539 441 533
www.brantwood.org.uk
Pencil Museum, Keswick:
01768 773 626
bit.ly/pencil-museum
Keswick Museum & Art Gallery, Keswick:
01768 773 263
www.keswickmuseum.org.uk
Tullie House Museum & Art Gallery, Carlisle:
01228 618 718
www.tulliehouse.co.uk

Tourist Information Centres

TICs can help with accommodation, local public transport, attractions and opening times. They also sell maps and guidebooks.

Ulverston no longer has a TIC but a Visitor Information Point at Market Hall, New Market Street, Ulverston, LA12 7LZ

Tourist Information Centre, Ruskin Avenue, Coniston, LA21 8EH,
01539 441 533
mail@conistontic.org

Tourist Information Centre, Market Cross, Ambleside, Cumbria, LA22 9BS,
01539 468 135
tic@thehubofambleside.com

Tourist Information Centre, Moot Hall, Keswick, Cumbria, CA12 5JR,
0845 901 0845
keswicktic@lake-district.gov.uk

Tourist Information Centre, Old Town Hall, Green Market, Carlisle, Cumbria, CA3 8JE,
01228 598 596,
tourism@carlisle.gov.uk